The How-To Guide for Nonfiction Writing

Lucy Calkins, Series Editor

Valerie Geschwind and Jennifer DeSutter

Photography by Peter Cunningham
Illustrations by Jennifer DeSutter

HEINEMANN ◆ PORTSMOUTH, NH

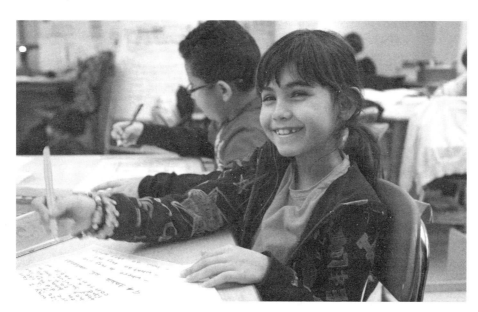

To Mom & Dad. For teaching me that this wild world is filled with raindrops on roses. —Valerie

To my students and colleagues, past and present. Thank you. —Jennifer

Heinemann
361 Hanover Street
Portsmouth, NH 03801–3912
www.heinemann.com

Offices and agents throughout the world

"Dedicated to Teachers" is a trademark of Greenwood Publishing Group, Inc.

The authors and publisher wish to thank those who have generously given permission to reprint borrowed material:

Figure 2–1: Cover of *Big Beasts: Kangaroo* used with permission of Saunders Book Company.

Session 4: Photo of writer's work spaces used with permission. Photo 1 by Isabel Huggan. Photo 2 by Pam Torres.

Cataloging-in-Publication data is on file with the Library of Congress.

ISBN-13: 978-0-325-08892-1

Editorial: Tracy Wells
Production: Elizabeth Valway, David Stirling, and Abigail Heim
Cover and interior designs: Jenny Jensen Greenleaf
Photography: Peter Cunningham
Composition: Publishers' Design and Production Services, Inc.
Manufacturing: Steve Bernier

Printed in the United States of America on acid-free paper
22 21 20 19 18   RWP   4 5 6 7 8 9

Acknowledgments

THIS UNIT HAS TRULY GROWN through the fullness of time. It has been piloted and developed, revised and rethought, tested and improved for years and years. It stands on the shoulders of many teachers and staff developers who have been doing this work alongside their second-graders for years. For that, we thank you.

This unit, as with all the units in the series, would not exist without Lucy Calkins. Thank you for your mentorship, both as a teacher and writer. You have taught us how to take ideas and spin them into meaningful prose, as you would fibers to yarn. Like the thousands of writers before us, both children and adults alike, who have learned to live a writerly life at your hand, we are forever grateful.

To our leaders and the Teachers College Reading and Writing Project (TCRWP), your vision is what gives us wings that bring this work into schools across New York City, the country, and the world. Amanda Hartman, who contributed to not only this unit, but to our staff development, by always asking the right questions. You have modeled for us what it means to live the life of an inquirer. Laurie Pessah, whose listening ear and magnanimous support gets us through each day. Kathleen Tolan, whose insightful wisdom helps us outgrow, not only our work with teachers, but ourselves. Mary Ehrenworth, who with every conversation helps us live today better than yesterday.

We couldn't imagine a greater team to learn and grow beside than the staff developers at the Project. We want to acknowledge the primary staff developers who are the most synergetic and selfless colleagues you'll find anywhere. Thank you, especially, to Katie Wears, Rachel Rothman, Brianna Parlitsis, Rebecca Cronin, Shanna Schwartz, Christine Holley, Katherine Cetrulo, Marie Mounteer, Allyse Jacobellis, and Dani Sturtz for your insights, expertise, and love. This book would not be half as graceful without Julia Mooney, who has taught us brevity and poise within our writing. You have been the connective tissue between words in the air and words on the page. Thank you.

We were blessed to have been writing this book alongside a few others in the series. As we ventured through this journey, the authors of those books have been there to both metaphorically and literally hold our hands. Thank you, Katie Clements, Liz Dunford, Mike Ochs, Brooke Geller, Alissa Levy, and Havilah Jespersen for walking, steadily, at our side.

The staff at Heinemann truly embodies the phrase, "It takes a village," and we feel lucky to be part of that village, if only temporarily. Thank you, Tracy Wells, for your thoughtful editing of this book. We appreciate the spirit you brought to our words and are grateful for the questions you asked that led us to greater precision. Abby Heim, for your patience and dedication, we are indebted to you.

While the class described in this unit is a composite class, with children gleaned from classrooms in very different contexts and put together here, there are particular teachers and students who piloted and contributed to this work. You brought each session to life and we are forever grateful. Thank to Dawn Sauro at Matunuck Elementary School, Kristi Smith, Caitlin Maulucci, and Jen Czaja from Carl Allgrove School and Joyce Rooks from Creekside Elementary School for putting your heart and soul into each session. To Monique Lopez-Paniagua and Irtis Gonzalez, leaders at PS 101Q for believing in this book and to your teachers, Allison Gorham, Erika Starr, Hillary Fiden, and Anna Ippolito, for making each session a reality. To Kristi Mraz at PS 59, for sharing your visions of a world in which we all teach each other what we know a lot about.

Lastly, to the future teachers of this book, we hope you have as much fun teaching this unit to your students as we had dreaming it up and writing it down for each of you.

—Valerie and Jennifer

Contents

BEND I   Writing Lots of Nonfiction Books Quickly

In this session, you'll teach children that nonfiction writers write around areas of expertise. When the topic is one they know well, they can start a book right away and write it quickly.

In this session, you'll teach children that nonfiction writers notice what other nonfiction writers have done in their books and think, "I can try this, too!"

In this session, you'll teach children that nonfiction writers can write more on each page. They do this by rereading and then thinking, "What else could I say?"

In this session, you'll teach children that writers get stronger by looking at their writing, setting goals, and making plans.

In this session, you could teach children that writers reread their writing as an editor, checking their spelling, grammar, and punctuation to make their piece easier for their readers to understand.

BEND II   Writing for an Audience

In this session, you'll teach children that when nonfiction writers are writing for an audience, they first think of who their audience will be and then write the information that audience would want to know.

In this session, you'll teach children that once nonfiction writers have considered who their audience will be and what information that audience would want to know, they think, "How can I help my readers picture the information?"

In this session, you'll teach children that nonfiction writers grab their audience's interest from the start of a chapter with an interesting lead.

BEND III Writing Nonfiction Books of All Kinds

 Registration instructions to access the digital resources that accompany this book may be found on p. xi.

Welcome to the Unit

WHEN YOU CLOSE YOUR EYES and picture your second-graders, chances are you see their puffed-up confidence as they stand tall, shoulders pushed back, walking down the hallway. Their inch-too-short sleeves and pant legs hitting their ankles only serve to bring attention to their fast-paced growth. Second-graders sling their backpacks over their shoulders with the ease of a big kid, with smiles that show off a mix of holey gaps and big, white, adult-sized teeth squeezed into still child-sized mouths.

Teachers of primary-aged students will *all* report that their young students are often bursting at the seams with information, eager to share their areas of expertise with anyone who will listen. Second-graders are no exception, yet they are special. They are a little bit bigger, a little bit older, and of course, have more schooling under their belts. They come to us able to line up with ease, shop for books in the classroom library without help, and sit on the rug, ready to learn. Just as our second-graders arrive with all of this knowledge about routines, they also come to us with a plethora of knowledge about how to teach others, how to write nonfiction.

This unit *The How-To Guide for Nonfiction Writing*, assumes that your second-graders bring knowledge of nonfiction writing with them, using it to springboard to new heights. Therefore the emphasis of this unit won't be on coming up with areas of expertise, structuring a book using a table of contents, or planning across pages. Your students will do those things, of course, but with independence. This unit will instead support students' endeavor in writing many books in shorter time frames, crafting information with a specific audience in mind, and helping students dive into an inquiry of other kinds of nonfiction texts, learning to teach information in different ways.

The How-To Guide for Nonfiction Writing sets writers up to teach about areas of personal expertise, and thus it is well positioned early on in second grade. This unit should serve as a prequel to *Lab Reports and Science Books*, Unit 2 in the second-grade Units of Study in Opinion, Information, and Narrative Writing series. *The How-To Guide for Nonfiction Writing* gives students the opportunity to lift the level of their nonfiction writing before diving into writing about science topics that are brand new. You will see your second-graders flourish as nonfiction writers, feeling even more confident as they jump into writing about unfamiliar topics later in the year.

To ensure that students are prepared for this next step, volume will be key. Now that second-graders feel strong enough to write long, they often stick with one book, filling it endlessly with pages and chapters. This unit encourages students to write long, but to do so across many books in each bend. Every time students begin a new book, they generate an idea, plan, and organize their book. The more practice students have moving through the writing process in this way, the more ease they will have each and every time they pick up a blank booklet from the writing center. Rallying students to write many books across this unit will set them up for success when they write during the *Lab Reports and Science Books* unit, and with every unit across the year.

There is another good reason to teach this unit early on in the year. If you are also teaching from the Units of Study for Teaching Reading series, you might choose to teach Unit 2, *Becoming Experts: Reading Nonfiction* alongside this unit. Whenever possible, it is helpful to make these reading-writing connections for your students. As kids dive into the world of reading nonfiction, it will only serve to strengthen their ability to write nonfiction and vice versa. You may also have just finished teaching *Lessons from the Masters* in which students learned to deeply study mentor texts, culling them for craft. With this newly developed skill set, students can be reminded that the nonfiction books they read, even during Reading Workshop, can serve as mentors for their writing.

Finally, this unit provides opportunities for independence like never before. Students will not only write nonfiction chapter books, standing on the shoulders of first grade, they will also explore many kinds of nonfiction books, trying on different structures with increased levels of autonomy. You will hand over the reins to your students as they choose among different kinds of nonfiction, study them alongside peers, and try them on while bringing forth all of their previous learning.

OVERVIEW OF THE UNIT

The unit ahead is divided into three bends. It begins with students writing nonfiction chapter books and then builds in sophistication as students move through Bend II, lifting the level of their nonfiction chapter books. The unit ends with students taking all they've learned over the course of the first two bends and writing different kinds of nonfiction books, with transference and independence as key goals. The first bend is short, giving your students an opportunity to remember all they know about writing nonfiction chapter books and giving them a chance to write, write, write—practicing across different books. Bend II teaches students to consider their audience, helping them write with purpose as they angle their books toward the information a specific audience would need to know. This bend is the longest and will be the one you'll want to spend the most time on, because it provides a lot of opportunity for elaboration and revision. The last bend, which hands the reins over to students as they make choices about how to shape their information and consider what kind of book to make, is six sessions long, though, as always, you should tailor it to your students and their needs.

Bend I: Writing Lots of Nonfiction Books Quickly

In the first bend, "Writing Lots of Nonfiction Books Quickly," students will begin to write nonfiction books with vigor right out of the gate. Students will use all they know to write many books, spending only a day or two on each book before moving on to a new one. To launch the unit you'll create suspense, directing children to the nonfiction section of the library and noting that none of *their* nonfiction books live on those shelves. The only way to remedy that is to begin writing nonfiction of their own! You'll let students know that if

they choose nonfiction topics on which they are already an expert, they can get started quickly.

This sets the course for all that lies ahead in the bend as you teach writers to study other nonfiction authors, noticing the interesting and cool things they do to teach in their books, and trying those moves on right away. Students will keep their book baggies close by as they search for craft moves they want to use. You'll also teach writers that as they reread, they might find that they can squeeze even more information out of their brains, teaching all they know about these expert topics.

Once students have a few books written, you'll want to teach them how to set goals using the Information Writing Checklist as a tool. As Bend I winds down, you'll coach writers to edit their books alongside you. The bend culminates with a celebration of the new nonfiction authors that have blossomed in your classroom as they write "about the author" pages and share favorite parts of their books with classmates.

Bend II: Writing for an Audience

The next bend, "Writing for an Audience," asks students to do just that. Your second-graders will now not only choose topics, but choose an audience as well, providing them with purpose and helping students to angle their writing toward a person or persons who will ultimately read their book. Teaching your students to write for audience allows them to be choosy with the information they put down on the page. For example, a book about bike riding for a kid sister would contain different information than if it were for a grandma. During this bend, you'll write a more developed demonstration text, which you'll angle toward a specific audience as well. This demonstration text will serve as both a model and a place for students to practice new skills alongside you.

You'll launch the second bend by inviting students to choose an audience and ask themselves, "What information does my audience want to know?" Your students will start off writing books keeping this question in mind, considering how to interest that audience, including writing descriptions and comparisons that will ultimately help their audience picture the information they are teaching. You'll lead students in an inquiry of a mentor text, helping them notice how a mentor author hooks readers right from the start of each chapter. Students will experiment with different chapter leads as they consider which will gain their readers' interest, keeping them on the edge of their seats. You'll give students lots of opportunity to rehearse their books with peers, as students turn classmates into a "practice audience," providing opportunities for feedback.

When writers have one or two books filled with information, they need to reread considering if they've answered all of their readers' questions. You'll teach writers the power of revision, supporting them as they add and take away information in places that would leave your audience confused or wanting more.

As you near the end of the bend, you'll remind writers to set goals for their writing once again, using the Information Writing Checklist, and then taking those goals across a book, from chapter to chapter before setting a new goals. Students will also spend extra time making sure that their writing is easy to read by attending to spelling, as they use words they know how to spell to correct misspelled words or write brand-new words. To celebrate, students will become book fairies! After fancying up their books to publish, they'll wrap one and gift it to their intended audience.

Bend III: Writing Nonfiction Books of All Kinds

At the start of the third bend, "Writing Nonfiction Books of All Kinds," you'll invite writers to shape expert information in new ways. You'll help them consider how the information they previously structured into a nonfiction chapter book could be worked into a question-and-answer book, a story that teaches, or a how-to book. Students will study mentors of these different kinds of nonfiction texts, first for structure.

You'll then remind students that using a mentor can help them solve problems and answer their own questions. With their classmates, writers will lead mentor inquiries, culling craft from nonfiction texts that they can then use in their own books. You'll remember all the while that students will approximate this new work as best they can, taking what they notice other authors have tried and trying it on in their own way. You'll also teach writers that it is of utmost importance to carry old learning into new books turning charts from preceding bends into "to-do" lists as a way of reminding themselves to incorporate that work into their new pieces.

The end of the bend is celebratory in nature. Hard work deserves recognition! You'll notice that we included a couple of sessions designed both to prepare for the celebration and to highlight the achievement of becoming nonfiction writers. Students will first work to provide each other with feedback leading up to the final days of the unit. Then, students will generate plans to prepare their books, making final touches using any resources from the unit that they choose.

The unit celebration sets up writers to hold a learning expo. You'll certainly want them to consider who to invite and provide the opportunity to make and send invitations to both families and classrooms around the school. On the day of the expo, you'll invite students to pick one published piece and consider, based on the type of book they wrote, how to celebrate the teaching inside of it. Stand back and watch with pride as your students independently plan for this celebration, coming up with creative ways to showcase their books. You'll be amazed at your students' poise during the expo, as your second-graders talk to invited guests about all they've learned.

ASSESSMENT

At the start of the school year, you will probably have assessed your students' information writing by conducting an on-demand performance assessment. If this is your second unit of study, you may decide not to conduct a second assessment just yet, postponing that second on-demand until the end of this unit. Of course, if you opted not to assess your students' information-writing skills at the beginning of the school year, or are using this unit as a stand-alone unit, then you will absolutely want to give an on-demand assessment before the unit begins.

If you are using this book as a part of your second-grade writing units of study, then you can look to *Writing Pathways: Performance Assessments and Learning Progressions, Grades K–8* for more detailed instructions about administering and scoring an on-demand writing assessment. There you will find a specific prompt for assessing your children's information writing. We hope you follow those guidelines so that the conditions under which you conduct the assessment are the same as those in other schools across the nation. But the really important thing is that you and your colleagues determine a single way in which all of you, as second-grade teachers, will administer the assessment. It is essential that the conditions are as similar across classrooms as you can manage so that you can compare the results.

If you are using this book as a stand-alone unit, then you will want to use this section and the Information Writing Checklist included in the online resources to help administer and score your writers' on-demands.

The prompt is:

"Think of a topic that you've studied or that you know a lot about. Tomorrow, you will have forty-five minutes to write an informational (or all-about) text that teaches others interesting and important information and ideas about that topic. If you want to find and use information from a book or another outside source to help you with this writing, you may bring that with you tomorrow. Please keep in mind that you'll have only this one period to complete this, so you'll need to plan, draft, revise, and edit in one sitting. Write in a way that shows all that you know about information writing."

You'll want to let your youngsters know that they can use the whole writing workshop (forty-five minutes) to write the best that they can and to fill their pages with as much information as they can teach. Provide students with five-page booklets in which to write, with space for a picture and several lines for writing. Because you will examine the work your children produce alongside a K–5 learning progression—or if you're using this book as a stand-alone unit alongside the first- and second-grade checklist—we recommend you give them some additional instructions for this task.

"In your writing, make sure you:

- Introduce the topic you will teach about
- Include lots of information
- Organize your writing
- Use transition words
- Write an ending."

This on-demand will give you a snapshot of your students' strengths and needs. At the start of second grade, you should expect that your students' writing will be roughly at the first-grade level, if they come from a strong writing curriculum. You will want to look closely at the work your students produce during the on-demand against the first- and second-grade Information Writing Checklists. You will want to pay particular attention to how students organize their writing and develop it to teach more across all of the pages. You will want to note the ways in which your writers use a five-page booklet as a planning and structuring tool, as well as their proficiency in generating an idea to write about and how they revise and edit. Observing students while

they write their on-demands will give you as much valuable information as the pieces themselves.

You will want to gather a few of the on-demands from your classroom and meet with your colleagues to study the work students produced. Part of assessing students' writing is studying it in the company of others to make plans for the unit ahead. To plan ways to tailor your instruction to your students, you will probably want everyone to bring examples of writing that represent levels 1, 2, 3, and 4 if you are using the rubric, or examples of writing reaching toward the first-grade Information Writing Checklist as well as the second-grade checklist. With your grade-level team, you may decide to bring the exemplars from *Writing Pathways* to the meeting and set those alongside the pieces you selected to study, or you may decide to create your own exemplars using the criteria of the rubric or checklist. Having exemplar pieces will help as you study and discuss your students' pieces with your colleagues. Assigning an exact level for each student is not as important as the conversations you have about the work. All students will have strengths in some areas, as well as areas of need. Paying attention to the data the on-demands provide will help you design small groups and maximize instruction during this upcoming unit.

You will notice opportunities across the unit for students to use the Information Writing Checklist to self-assess, set goals, and to develop action plans for their work. Students will be able to see for themselves what writing skills they already have that they'll carry into this unit, as well as some skills toward which they'll reach. If your students used the Information Writing Checklist in kindergarten and first grade, they will notice the ways in which the checklists stay the same (the indicators across the top and side), as well as how the checklist changes (the specific grade-level descriptors). If your students are newer to using checklists, and specifically the one used in this unit, you can support them by studying the descriptors alongside a piece of writing, so that they can notice specifically how information writers structure and develop their pieces. The descriptors on each checklist will be particularly useful as you and your students discuss and plan for their goals. We suggest that students keep a copy of the checklist inside their folders as well as their on-demand so that they can keep tabs on their progress from the very beginning of the unit until the end. They can notice both how they've grown as nonfiction writers and what they can do to get even stronger.

At the end of the unit, you'll give the on-demand assessment again, using the same prompt to invite students to write another on-demand information text. You will be able to lay the two on-demands side by side and mark them up, annotating the ways that each student has grown.

GETTING READY

As you prepare for the unit, think about the materials your students will need as writers of nonfiction books. If you taught the first unit in the second-grade Units of Study in Opinion, Information, and Narrative Writing series, *Lessons from the Masters*, you will already have a writing center filled with a variety of booklet choices as well as revision strips, Post-its®, scissors, tape, staplers, and extra pens. If this is the first unit of study in writing for you and your students, you will want to gather the aforementioned materials into a space in your classroom where they are easily accessible to all your students. Across the unit, students will need access to new booklets as well as revision materials, and they'll work most efficiently if they do not have to wait for you to distribute these materials. Your writing center should also include a variety of paper choices for students to choose from. For examples of paper choices, please look to the online resources. Generally, teachers will provide three to four kinds of paper choice with a varying number of lines and pages stapled into booklets, as well as loose sheets of the same kinds of paper. Be sure to include a Table of Contents paper choice. In Bend III, students will create different kinds of nonfiction books, from how-to books to question-and-answer books. They can certainly continue to use the same paper choices from earlier bends, but we also recommend that you offer up blank paper so students are free to plan and structure their books as they see fit.

In addition to a writing center, your writers will each need a writing folder to house their books as they work across the unit. Again, if you taught *Lessons from the Masters*, students will be familiar with using folders, and they can empty them of their narrative writing for a fresh start as nonfiction writers. We generally recommend a two-pocket folder with one side marked and reserved for "in-progress writing" and the other side reserved for "done for now" pieces. Across the unit you will note that students use Post-its several times—to make plans, give feedback, and mark up texts—so it is helpful for each writer to have a small stack of Post-its tucked inside the pocket of his or her folder. You'll also want to prepare Tiny Topic notepads for students to use as a place to collect topics.

You will also find it helpful to plan for the number of books students will produce across the unit so that you can keep a pulse on writers' volume and stamina. The way writers improve is through repeated practice; therefore, we recommend students aim to write two to three pieces in each bend, for a total of six to nine pieces in the whole unit. The books that students write in Bend I will be more draft-like as they work to warm up their nonfiction writing muscles, while the books they create in Bend II will be more developed. Then in Bend III, we recommend that students try more than one different kind of book so that they really get to flex their nonfiction writing muscles.

In addition to preparing for the writing your students will do across the unit, you will also want to prepare for the work they will do with mentor texts. In Bend I, you'll introduce writers to some familiar nonfiction authors such as Gail Gibbons and Seymour Simon, so you may want to have a few of their books on hand. As always, feel free to choose other favorite nonfiction authors your students may be familiar with. In Session 2 you invite writers to study nonfiction texts of their own choosing. If your students are not reading nonfiction at this time, you will want to plan for writers to spend a bit of time during Reading Workshop choosing texts and reading them in preparation for this session. Then in Bend II, we use the text *Extreme Sports* by Sean Finnegan to highlight the ways in which writers hook their readers. You can of course choose another mentor text your writers may be more familiar with to study.

During the final bend, students will shift from writing all-about books to writing different kinds of nonfiction, such as how-to books, question-and-answer books, and stories that teach. You'll want to gather a small stack of each kind to have on hand across the bend so that writers have plenty of books to study. We recommend books such as *How to Be a Baby by Me, the Big Sister* by Sally Lloyd-Jones as a how-to mentor text, *Why Do Dogs Bark?* by Joan Holub as a question-and-answer mentor, and *Growing Frogs* by Vivien French as a mentor of a story that teaches. Additionally, before this third bend begins, you may want to use a bit of your read-aloud time to start to familiarize students with the kinds of texts they will create in Bend III. For a list of recommended nonfiction books, see the online resources in Session 14.

Finally, it is important to imagine the kind of writing your students will be doing across the unit and to create pieces that you can use during your minilessons, conferences, and small groups. You may even want to create these in the same kind of booklets your students will use to write their own books, so that these feel to kids like true models of what they themselves write. Certainly you will want to create a bare-bones writing piece that could be used in several different ways for revision. This piece may be a booklet with a sentence or two on each page. In this case, we recommend you copy this piece so that you can use it in a variety of ways. Your writing is a key element for supporting writers throughout the unit.

ONLINE DIGITAL RESOURCES

A variety of resources to accompany this unit are available in the online resources, including charts and examples of student work shown throughout *The How-To Guide for Nonfiction Writing*, as well as links to other electronic resources. Offering daily support for your teaching, these materials will help you provide a structured learning environment that fosters independence and self-direction.

To access and download all the digital resources for this unit:

1. Go to **www.heinemann.com** and click the link in the upper right to log in. (If you do not have an account yet, you will need to create one.)
2. **Enter the following registration code** in the box to register your product: WUOS_NWDY2.
3. Under **My Online Resources**, click the link for *The How-To Guide for Nonfiction Writing*.

The digital resources are available under the headings; click a file name to download.

(You may keep copies of these resources on up to six of your own computers or devices. By downloading the files you acknowledge that they are for your individual or classroom use and that neither the resources nor the product code will be distributed or shared.)

Launching the Big Work of Nonfiction Writing in Accessible Ways

IN THIS SESSION, you'll teach children that nonfiction writers write around areas of expertise. When the topic is one they know well, they can start a book right away and write it quickly.

GETTING READY

✔ Students' narrative writing from *Lessons from the Masters* (if you taught that unit), placed in baskets in the fiction section of your classroom library (see Connection)

✔ An empty basket, labeled with your class's room number, to place in the nonfiction section of your classroom library (see Connection)

✔ A stack of blank booklets to place at the center of each table (see Link)

✔ Students' writing folders (see Share)

✔ A book by Seymour Simon and one by Gail Gibbons along with their photographs, or those of two other children's nonfiction authors you will reference (see Share)

THIS SESSION launches the upcoming unit on nonfiction writing by helping kids feel as if writing nonfiction books can be "no big deal." The goal is to make kids comfortable writing nonfiction and to help them become accustomed to cranking out a lot of nonfiction books, working with considerable independence and confidence.

You will not see an emphasis on elaboration, on writing in ways that rally readers' interest or that answer readers' questions. All of that will come in time. Your first intention is to get kids into the swing of thinking up topics for nonfiction books, choosing one and getting started writing, then generating ideas of a few different chapters for that book, and writing more than one chapter. It will be important to make sure that kids are independent as writers of nonfiction.

This unit starts in this manner because too often second-graders work for a week or even for a whole unit on one giant nonfiction book. Each step in that process takes a very long time, with teachers and kids working toward an image of perfection. The problem is that perfection from a seven-year-old means that the work isn't done by that youngster alone. The only way to get perfection is for *you* to do most of the work. Meanwhile, kids need tons of repeated practice, and they need opportunities to ratchet up the level of their work, one step at a time, so their work gets better over time.

So today, you teach kids that nonfiction writers have a choice. They *could* write nonfiction books about topics on which they know very little, but in those instances, the process of writing can stretch across a great deal of time. But they can also write on topics on which they already have expertise, and in those instances, writers can write quickly. And you rally your youngsters to start doing just that: a book a day!

Launching the Big Work of Nonfiction Writing in Accessible Ways

CONNECTION

Convene the writers quickly and create an aura of excitement around the upcoming, still secret new unit by rallying students to write their own nonfiction books to add to the library.

"Writers, come quickly because today is a big day. We're starting a whole new unit—our second in the year—so let's not waste a single moment."

The children gathered quickly, with a buzz in the air. "Before we get started thinking about the sorts of books you'll be writing in this next unit," I said, "will you think for a minute about how super-cool it is that you are now authors? You've published your first books this year, haven't you? And those books are now in our library for anyone to read. Can you see where your published books from Unit 1 are? That's right! They are in the narrative section of our library, because they are all narratives, all stories.

"But writers, here's the thing. When I put your books there, alongside other books by authors you love (by Jane Yolen and Angela Johnson and Mo Willems and the rest), I couldn't help but notice that there is a whole other section to our library that doesn't yet have any books by class 203B!"

I gestured to the nonfiction section of the library, and kids called out, "The nonfiction part!" "The true books!" "The science books!"

I nodded as I pointed again to the nonfiction section of the library. "You are right. This class hasn't yet written any books for the *nonfiction* part of our library, the part of the library that contains true books about science and history and the whole wide wonderful world. So, writers, I'm wondering, are you game to devote this unit to doing some nonfiction writing?"

The kids nodded, and I added an empty (but inviting) basket to the nonfiction shelf in the library, and said, "So let's set a goal. By the end of today, let's start filling this basket up with books by Raymond and Josh and Gayle and Emma and all the rest of you. Let me see you rolling up your sleeves, because we have work to do!" I rolled up my imaginary sleeves.

If you did not teach Lessons from the Masters: Improving Narrative Writing *from the Units of Study in Opinion, Information, and Narrative Writing, your students may not have written narrative books to include in your classroom library. If that is the case, you might adapt this connection by focusing right away on building kids' excitement about writing nonfiction books for your library. Either way, you'll want to keep the unit a surprise up until this point to build suspense and excitement for students.*

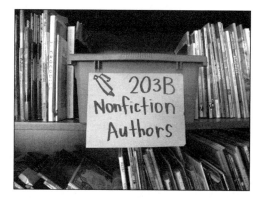

FIG. 1–1 An empty book basket with a class number attached waits for future nonfiction books.

Name the teaching point.

"Writers, today I want to teach you that nonfiction writers write about topics on which they have expertise. Sometimes writers choose a brand-new topic, and spend a *long* time getting to be an expert on that topic. But other times, nonfiction writers choose a topic on which they are *already* expert, in which case they get started right away."

TEACHING

Rally kids' energy by talking up the way the books they write can soon go into each other's book baggies to be read during reading workshop.

"Remember, writers, your goal is to write some nonfiction books that we can put into that basket in our library right away. Who knows, during reading workshop, some of you might even take books from this basket to put in your book baggies!"

Ask whether one child could whip up a book on some unfamiliar topic. After eliciting a no, generate a list of topics on which that child *could* whip up quick nonfiction books.

"So if Raymond wants to write a book right now, today, do you think it would be a good idea for him to write a book about . . . um . . . about the settlements that people are making on Antarctica?" I pointed to that part of the globe.

The kids chimed, "No!"

"Okay, okay. What if Raymond decided to write a book about Neptune (you know, that planet that is way, way out there past Saturn)? Raymond, here's a pen. Can you get started writing *All about Neptune*?" Raymond laughed, and shook his head.

"You are right. Those would make dandy nonfiction books and I would definitely want to read them, but if Raymond wants to get a whole book written today to go in the nonfiction section of our library, it has got to be about a topic he *already* knows a lot about. So Pedro, you're Raymond's pal. I'm going to give you and Raymond twenty seconds, and in that amount of time, will you two list *three* things that Raymond could write about—today? Writers, as you watch Pedro and Raymond, you might also begin to list topics on your fingers that you could write a whole nonfiction book about today!"

Soon Raymond and Pedro had agreed on a short list. Raymond could write about baseball, about skateboarding, or about the local ice cream shop.

Recap in ways that accentuate the transferable skills you just demonstrated.

"Writers, I'm hoping that as you watched Raymond and Pedro generate a list of topics that Raymond could write a nonfiction book about, you came up with a list of topics that *you* could write about as well. And I'm hoping that this

Choose a child who is famous for his or her obsessions. This will be the child who adores baseball or horses or dinosaurs or video games. This should also be a child who has some confidence as a writer.

If the children seem to have trouble generating topics super quickly, you can say to the class, "Remember those game shows that have the audience give hints? Let's give them some hints. What about if we suggest they think about a sport? What if we suggest they think about a pet? A TV show? A place they like to go?"

helped you realize that the way writers come up with ideas for nonfiction books they can write quickly is by thinking, 'What are the topics I know really well, on which I am an expert?'"

ACTIVE ENGAGEMENT

Recruit children's help finding a topic that you could write about today. Demonstrate this by first suggesting topics for yourself that *won't* work—because you would need to first research them.

"So you helped Raymond come up with a topic that he could write about today—in the next half hour. Will you do that for me as well? Like, for example, I hear that some people have wild animals as pets. Someone told me that there are people who have *hippos* as pets! Do you think I could pick up my pen right now and write a whole book on people who have hippos as pets? No?" I said in response to kids shaking their heads.

"Here is another topic. What about this? I heard once that some people are developing cars that drive themselves. There doesn't have to be a person in the driver's seat. Honest! Do you think I could pick up my pen and write a book about cars that drive themselves? No?" I said again. "You are right.

Notice that the details are what make this entertaining and engaging. You'll be suggesting outlandish topics, crazy topics, and the detail and specificity of what you say will keep kids engaged.

Ask students to brainstorm topics you could write about. Voice over as children talk in a way that also helps them imagine topics that might be good for *them*.

"So you guys know a lot about me. Will you think about what I know about, and see if you can help me come up with a topic that I could write about this very day? Turn and talk. Work together to help me find a topic. Go!"

As the children talked, I voiced over. "I'm wondering if there might be a sport or a game that I know a lot about. Hmm, . . ." Then another minute later, "I'm wondering if there might be a place? A pet? A kind of food?"

After another minute, I said, "Time's up. So, writers, I'm dying to hear your ideas for the writing I could do. If you have ideas, whisper them into your hand." I leaned in, cupping my ear toward the class, catching their ideas for my writing.

LINK

Send children off to begin writing and remind them that the goal is to finish a book today.

"It is time for your writing. You've all helped me—now help yourselves. Give me a thumbs up if you have an idea for one thing you could write a nonfiction book about." Most of the class so signaled.

"If a few of you need help, stick around and you can help each other like you helped me. Meanwhile, I've put a stack of blank books at the center of each table—get started. And remember, the goal is to finish a book today so that we can have a basket full of nonfiction books by class 203B."

Before sending your students off of the rug, it is helpful to know that they are ready to dive right into writing. Having kids physically signal that they are eager to head off is a great way of assessing who is ready to write and who needs a few more moments to think and help from you.

Rallying Independence *and* Excitement

ONE OF THE MOST INSPIRING ASPECTS of this unit is that it asks children to share their passions, their interests, their lives with others—something they are dying to do with anyone who will listen! Most of your youngsters are happy to hold court on a topic with their friends—so your goal will be to help them do that on paper. If you can tap into their eagerness to share, then the work of generating a topic and setting out to write all about it will be second nature to your second-graders.

Today's conferring and small-group work will be especially important because you are rallying youngsters to participate with great energy in the work of this unit. To make best use of your time, it will help if you think in advance about some of the teaching methods you will use and some of the content you will teach.

Use table conferences to reach many writers.

Because all your students would profit from a supportive nudge today, you will probably rely on small groups more than one-to-one conferring. At the start of a unit, the needs of kids are not especially differentiated yet, because everyone is at the very beginning. Therefore, many teachers find that it is efficient to lead table conferences with one tableful of youngsters after another.

FIG. 1–2   Lily uses sketches to help teach different parts of her topic across pages.

To do this, pull up to a table and take a look at what writers are doing. As you look over the children's work, notice if one writer is doing something that you wish everyone were doing (each in his or her own way). If you spot something, you can rally the group to notice what their classmate has done, and you can suggest they might all try similar work. For example, if a writer has sketched a few items in the corner of her page, and after writing a sentence or two seems to go back to the sketch of items, crossing one off as completed, you'll definitely want to say, "Oh my goodness! Writers, will you look at the system Samantha has built for herself? She started her page by thinking of what she might write about, rehearsing for her writing. She didn't just pick up her pen and start writing—no way! She instead *thought*. She thought, 'What do I know about

---

MID-WORKSHOP TEACHING   **Adding Chapters to a Nonfiction Book**

After just a very few minutes of time, I interrupted. "Writers, can I stop you? I know you haven't had much time at all but I'm noticing the coolest thing and wanted to mention it. *Some* of you are making chapters inside your books, just like you did in first grade, and that is totally cool. Andrew, for example, is writing about soccer (surprise, surprise) and one of his chapters is called 'How to Score,' and another one is called 'Two Positions.'

"If you just plunged in and started writing, that's not a problem. Read over what you have written and see if you can come up with a title for that chapter. Then, if you want to jump to a different thing that is still about your topic, just make a different chapter title on top of the next page. It's easy-peasy!"

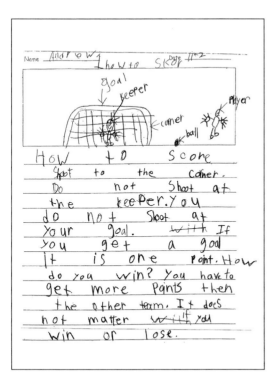
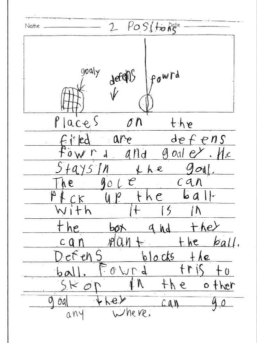
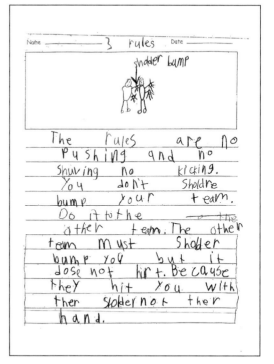

FIG. 1–3   Andrew first sketched pictures to plan his book and then wrote each chapter.

this?' and then she drew a few quick pictures to remind her of those things. Now she is writing about one of her items, then crossing it off, then writing about the next. It would be *so cool* if there were another writer at this table who might try Samantha's strategy of rehearsing for writing, planning for writing, making little sketches to hold those plans! I'm wondering, if maybe, maybe, another writer at this table just might try something similar. That would be so terrific!" You could tell the kids you need to work with another table, and walk away—fully confident that they'd all try Samantha's strategy.

Perhaps you will see another writer rereading what he had written, and you could ask, "Are you rereading as a way to get ideas for what *more* you could say? Are you? I do the exact same thing when I'm writing. That is such a grown-up strategy." Then you could ask the other writers to give you their attention. "Eyes up here," you could say, and after the writers have all paused in their work and given you their full attention (it is worth waiting) you could say, "I'm not sure you are aware of the smart work others at this table are doing. For example, I just saw Reginald doing something *so* smart. It might seem like a little thing, but it is actually *huge*. Let me tell you what he did,

because maybe some of the rest of you would be willing to try it. Reginald wrote a few lines and then he didn't have more to say. But do you think he just turned the page and jumped to a new page? *No!* Instead, he reread what he wrote, knowing that by doing so, more ideas would come. And sure enough, after he reread, he got more ideas and wrote three more lines!"

In some of your table conferences, you won't be building off what one writer has done, but will instead be issuing a tip. You might say, "Writers, I know you have tons of ideas about your topic. Don't teach them all on one page! Remember that when you are done writing about one thing, go to another page."

Resist the urge to solve all the small problems that arise during the first days of a new unit. Instead, highlight and extol the independent and productive strategies you catch writers using across the workshop: utilizing the writing center or spelling resources, looking at charts for transferable strategies from the last unit, or holding quick partner conferences when they run into trouble. The fact is the genre of writing has changed in this unit from the last one, but writing workshop hasn't!

Meeting Nonfiction Authors

Ask students to turn and talk about nonfiction authors they love.

"Writers, can I stop you? I've placed your writing folders at your tables. Please bring it with you along with your writing from today, and let's gather at the meeting area to talk." As writers began to find their spots at the rug I said, "When you get here, will you show your partner how much you wrote today? Is your book ready to go into our library?"

The children convened and began immediately to open their books and show their partners the pages they'd written. I looked expectantly from book to book, but knew full well that the writers would need another day to continue writing. Their nonfiction pieces would remain in their folders for now.

Interrupting them, I said, "Writers, we talked earlier today about how your narrative writing is here in the library, right beside the books written by your favorite narrative authors—people like Mo Willems and Jane Yolen and Maurice Sendak. Now your nonfiction books will be going right alongside the books by your favorite *nonfiction* authors. I want to put your books right near those mentor nonfiction books, so will you tell me, who *are* your favorite nonfiction authors?"

I gestured for kids to hold in their thoughts—to just think silently—even though I knew that chances were good that most of them had no names at all surfacing in their minds. "Okay, go! Tell your partner the names of your favorite nonfiction authors."

Introduce students to two nonfiction authors. Share quick biographies and photos of them.

The room was almost silent. "Whoa, whoa, whoa! Hold on!" I said. "Just a minute! Do you mean to say that you haven't yet fallen in love with nonfiction authors?! Really? We have got to change that for sure.

"To write nonfiction, you are going to have to learn from nonfiction authors, because that's what *you* will be, right? I mean, when you want to be a dancer, you watch 'Dancing with the Stars.' When you want to be a teacher, you watch the most fabulous teacher in the world." I took a pretend bow. "So let's end today by learning just a little bit about a few nonfiction authors.

"Let me introduce you to Seymour Simon, for starters." I showed his picture on the document camera. "Listen to some things about him. First off, Seymour Simon is the author of more than 250 science books! Two hundred fifty books. He has written about faraway topics such as outer space, as well as close-by topics like the human heart. His favorite topic,

If you taught Lessons from the Masters: Improving Narrative Writing from the Units of Study in Opinion, Information, and Narrative Writing, prior to teaching this unit, your students should be quite familiar with the routine of meeting with a partner during the share to quickly review their writing with one another. If you have not already developed these routines, you may want to create writing partnerships before today's workshop and then take a few moments to model sharing writing with a partner from your class.

We chose two well-known nonfiction authors, Seymour Simon and Gail Gibbons, to introduce to students, though there are hundreds of nonfiction authors living right in your libraries! Feel free to choose your favorites, do a bit of research, and then teach your kids all about them and their writing lives.

though, is space. When he was a kid he belonged to an astronomy club and built his own telescope. He has written a *whole lot* of books on space—and you could do the same thing, writing a lot of books about the topic that is most important to you.

"Now, let me introduce you to Gail Gibbons!" I displayed her picture on the document camera as I held up a copy of one of her books. "When she was a young girl, she was always curious about how things work. She was so curious about clocks that one day she took a clock apart to study the insides of it! She ended up writing a book about it—*Clocks and How They Go*. I'm wondering if anyone in this room is like Gail Gibbons—interested in how things work and willing to find out on your own by taking something apart and studying the insides of it.

"Writers, are you ready to become nonfiction authors like these writers?" I pointed to Simon and Gibbons. "I know that during reading time, you are reading nonfiction books. Would you notice the author of those books? See if you can read 'about the author' sections and learn more things about the life of a nonfiction author."

Session 2

Learning from the Experts
Noticing, Naming, and Trying Out
Craft Moves in Nonfiction Books

TODAY you again convey to your students that they can write nonfiction books for the classroom library. But today you especially develop the idea that your kids will be joining the ranks of nonfiction authors the world over. They will be doing work that is not unlike the work that Seymour Simon does, and Melissa Stewart and Jean Craighead George.

To accentuate the reading-writing connection, you'll invite kids to study a nonfiction book they admire, noticing something the author has done that they could try as well. For now, your goal is not to channel kids to notice particularly important aspects of nonfiction texts. Instead, your goal is simply to remind your students that when they want to make their nonfiction books be the best they can be, it helps to look at a published book they admire and to think, "What has this author done that I could try?" and then to give that a try.

It is easier for kids to borrow from a mentor text if this borrowing happens during revision, so today's minilesson invites kids to revise yesterday's writing by adding whatever it is they admire.

The session ends with you reintroducing Tiny Topic notepads to students during the share. Tiny Topics notepads are another resource, like mentor texts, that students who experienced *Lessons from the Masters* will be familiar with. They are a tool to help kids gather ideas for the many books they will write. They also serve as a way to apprentice students to the life of living like a writer. They can carry their notepads around jotting down topics, just like professional writers do.

If your class has yet to use Tiny Topics notepads, you can introduce them today. Many teachers use mini spiral notepads, but you could also cut some loose-leaf pages and staple a stack together. Both versions do the trick!

IN THIS SESSION, you'll teach children that nonfiction writers notice what other nonfiction writers have done in their books and think, "I can try this, too!"

GETTING READY

✔ By the beginning of this session, students should have written or be almost finished with one book and be ready to begin a second one. For tips on supporting your students in increasing their writing volume, see the Conferring and Small-Group Work section.

✔ Student writing folders, containing the books they began writing in Session 1, and book baggies from reader's workshop filled with the nonfiction books students are reading (see Connection, Teaching, and Active Engagement)

✔ The empty basket, labeled with your class's room number, which you will place in the nonfiction section of your classroom library to receive students' nonfiction writing (see Connection)

✔ One student's writing from Session 1 and a nonfiction book from that same student's book baggie (see Teaching)

✔ "Nonfiction Writers" anchor chart (see Link)

✔ A stack of Post-its at each table (see Mid-Workshop Teaching)

✔ Tiny Topics notepads (see Share)

Learning from the Experts
Noticing, Naming, and Trying Out Craft Moves in Nonfiction Books

CONNECTION

Exult over the books that your children wrote, remind them that these books will soon be in the nonfiction section of your library, and point out that children will now read nonfiction as insiders.

"Writers, will you bring your folders and—listen carefully—your *book baggies* with you and meet me at the meeting area?"

Once the kids had gathered, I put the basket labeled "Nonfiction Authors of 203B" on my lap. "You did some really nice writing yesterday," I said. "So I have this bin here, and I was thinking we could put your writing into it." I motioned for the children sitting close by my feet to pass me their writing. "We're going to have some hot new books in our library. I bet you can't wait until reading workshop when you get to choose one of these to read." I read a few titles aloud: "*Basketball* by Liam, *All about Ice Cream* by Felix, and *Shopkins* by Xin Yi!

"When we began our unit yesterday, all of the books that you had written were stories. Now that has changed. It is a big deal that your books are going to be in the nonfiction section of the library."

❖ **Name the teaching point.**

"Today I want to teach you that once a person has written nonfiction books—once a person is an author of nonfiction books—that person's *reading* of nonfiction is forever changed. Authors of nonfiction books read books written by other authors and think, 'Whoa! Look what he did in his book! Look what she did! I should try that.'"

FIG. 2–1 A writer brings her book baggie filled with nonfiction books and writing folder to the meeting area.

Y[...]
e[...]
th[...]
th[...]

O[...]
bu[...]
ha[...]
bo[...]
in [...] you will need to return that writing to the authors. This is just being done to signal that the class's writing will end up as books they'll read.

[handwritten note:] ✗
C. Remind about N.F. & How they can help you.

TEACHING

Liken the work children will do to the work they did previously when they mentored themselves to authors of fiction. Emphasize that it is rare for kids to study the craft of nonfiction authors.

"What I just told you isn't really something new, is it? I mean, in our first unit of this year, you all read the authors of stories and thought, 'I should try that!'

"But here is something that you may not know. *Lots* of kids study the ways that authors write stories and then try to write in just those same ways. But for some very strange reason, most seven-year-olds don't study *nonfiction* books in the same way. It is true! Most seven-year-olds don't even have any nonfiction mentor-authors. So the work you are going to do today is important."

Set students up to help one child in the class notice things in a nonfiction mentor text that she can try out in her own writing.

"Right now, will all of you take out a nonfiction book that you like from your reading baggie?" As the kids pulled out books, I added. "Take out the book you wrote yesterday as well." I quickly redistributed the books I had collected earlier from the writers closest to me as other writers took their books from their folders.

Taking hold of Sasha's writing and the book she'd pulled from her reading baggie, I said, "Sasha, I'm going to borrow the nonfiction book you chose and the nonfiction book you wrote." Holding them up, I said, "Class, let's pretend for a minute that the book Sasha chose and the book that she wrote belong to all of us. Let's see if we can read the book she has chosen like nonfiction writers read nonfiction—we'll notice what the author has done and think, 'Whoa! We could try that same thing in our writing!' (Only remember, we are pretending Sasha's writing is ours.) Sasha, what is your writing about?"

I opened the booklet Sasha had written the day before and read, "Kittens." I quickly read through the first page, showing it to the children:

> Kittens are cute and cuddly. They are super soft and fuzzy. They have tiny paws.

Then, as if utterly perplexed, I held up the book Sasha had pulled from her reading baggie and looked between the two books—one on kittens, the other on volcanoes. "Wait! You're writing a book about *kittens* . . . How will this book about *volcanoes* give you ideas for your writing about *kittens*?" I gave the class a quizzical look.

The kids, of course, were on their knees, calling out that she could still learn stuff from the volcano book. "Let's try, right? Because what Sasha wants to do is what each one of you will be trying to do as well. You probably have the same deal as Sasha's: you wrote about one topic, and the book you are going to study is about a whole different topic. But you guys think that's okay, that you can still learn?

As we write this book, the TCRWP has been collecting names of favorite authors from teachers to develop state-of-the-art libraries, and the fascinating thing to us has been realizing that relatively few teachers have favorite nonfiction authors or books. When we ask for recommended nonfiction books, teachers tend to mention high-interest topics or publishers, not specific texts.

Even though students have prior experience using mentor texts, we find it is often helpful to remind them that they are looking for transferable writing moves and not to transfer the topic of the text. We've tucked this in here to help kids angle their thinking toward noticing these moves.

"Let's see what the author of this volcano book has done that Sasha might try in her kitten book. Writers, give me a thumbs up if you notice anything in this book that could help Sasha with hers."

I opened the volcano book to a page, which I showed the children. Hands shot up. I calmed them.

"Maybe you will see more than one thing Sasha could try," I said, signaling for them to keep thinking, to keep looking.

Then I pointed to Liam and said, "What's one thing?" and he pointed to the diagram of a volcano. Nodding, I said, "So you think Sasha could add a diagram? Would it be of a volcano?" The kids laughed at that silly idea, and I said, "You are right. She could add a diagram—perhaps of a kitten.

"Writers, can I add one more tip onto this? Try to notice not only *what* the author has done that you admire, but also *how* the author has done that. All of you, look at the diagram on this page and think, 'How did the author make a diagram? What tips could Sasha get from studying the author's diagram?'"

After half a minute of silence, I said, "Did some of you notice that she labeled the diagram? And used little lines to point to things? And has a caption?"

"Sasha, do you think you could do all those things as you add a diagram to your kitten book?" Sasha nodded enthusiastically.

Debrief, reminding writers that the work is transferable to other days and other books.

"Absolutely you could! Just like when you wrote stories and learned craft techniques from authors of fiction, you can learn from nonfiction book authors in the same way. You can read books written by nonfiction authors and think, 'Whoa! Look what he did in his book! I should try that.'"

ACTIVE ENGAGEMENT

Set partners up to study the nonfiction books in their baggies together, as writers do, noticing things they can try out in their own writing.

"Let's see what else you can learn! Right now, take the nonfiction book you chose from your baggie. Turn to your partner and start studying. As you and your partner look across your books, make sure you are studying like a writer. Notice all the cool things the author is doing that you could try in your own writing. Are you ready, partners? Go!"

As partners faced each other and began talking, I moved among them, listening in. "This book has a cool facts page," Felix pointed out to his partner.

In a voiceover, I called, "Don't forget to notice *how* the author has done that terrific thing."

You will choose a student from your class for this part of the minilesson. Your student will, of course, have his or her own book he or she has been writing and a nonfiction book pulled from the baggie. While any book from the reading baggie will work, you will want to notice that the featured element later on in the minilesson is a diagram. We chose this text feature because it is familiar, fun, and easily transferred to other books the children are writing.

Notice that I'm emphasizing the work of not only naming what the author is doing but also encouraging students to look more closely and study more precisely how the author has done this. Asking what and how are typical ways to help students inquire around a text. These questions help writers to clarify and name the transferable strategies from mentor texts, thus making it easier for them to bring the work into their own writing.

Invite children to now find places in their writing where they can try the work they noticed from their nonfiction reading books.

"So, ready to give this a go? Open up your folders and pull out the book you began yesterday. Think about what you just noticed in your reading book and find a place you could try it in your writing book. I'll know you have a plan for your book when I see you pointing."

I gave them a few seconds to do this, then said, "Ah, some of you are pointing to a *few* places—yes, you can try this work in more than one spot!"

Debrief by helping kids to see that what you have just taught them to do—rereading nonfiction texts as mentor texts—is something they can do whenever they are writing nonfiction.

"Writers, I know from now on every time you pick up a nonfiction book, you will not only read it to learn new information, but you will *also* read it to notice what the author has done as a writer. You will say to yourself, 'Whoa! Look what he did in his book! Look what she did! How did the writer do that?' And you'll think, 'I should try that.'"

LINK

Remind children that there is an entire library of nonfiction books they can study to improve their writing. Use today's teaching to start an anchor chart for the bend.

"Writers, before you head off to work today, I just want to remind you that we have a whole library filled with books by nonfiction authors, ready to be explored. Any time you want to improve your writing you can pick up a book and study it, asking, 'What has the author done that I could try?' And once you've noticed something helpful, like you did today, you can put it into practice right away. Off you go, writers!"

> ANCHOR CHART
>
> Nonfiction Writers
>
> • Read books by other writers and think "I could try that!"

Later on in the unit, you will support students in making more sophisticated choices about which writing moves to try, where, and why, but for now it is sufficient for them to notice and transfer strategies as best they can.

Translating "Author Moves" into More Writing

BECAUSE IT IS EARLY IN THE UNIT, today you will continue the work you began yesterday of rallying writers into the big work of the unit. Yesterday your conferring and small-group work nudged writers to tap into the topics on which they are experts. You reminded kids that writing nonfiction books is not any different than teaching others all about a topic. Kids love to teach about baseball and baby sisters and the latest TV series, and this unit will tap into their natural urge to teach others.

In the previous session, you coached kids to draw sketches to remind themselves of the subtopics they might address, to reread to prime their pump so they have more to add to a text, and to remember that when they've written all they know about one part of a topic, they can shift to addressing another part of that topic. All of that instruction will continue to be important today. This bend of the unit is all about rallying kids to write—and to write a lot.

Today's minilesson, however, shone a spotlight not on the content, but on the craft of nonfiction writing. The minilesson said to kids: "You can study a published book not only to learn more information to put into your book, but also to notice totally cool things that an author has done that you are game to try." This means that your teaching today will encompass not only the content, but also the craft of books.

The goal of today's teaching is not to be sure kids' work improves in any particular way. Instead, the session aims simply to channel writers to read differently because they are writers, noticing the craft moves other authors have made, and thinking about *how* they are writing, too. In this way, today's teaching continues to position youngsters as avid and productive writers of nonfiction. It helps them to know that people don't just live differently when they write, people also *read* differently.

The good news is that today's teaching builds on a great deal of prior work. Your kids already know how to study the author's craft in narrative texts, so you are simply reminding them to continue to do that work now that they are in a nonfiction unit of study.

Use small groups and conferences to channel writers to shift between reading and writing, between revising their illustrations and revising their sentences.

You may find some children who are far more interested in the visual features in the books they read and in those they write than they are in the written texts. There is a lot to be learned by studying diagrams and illustrations, so refrain from a knee-jerk reaction because you can certainly support this work. You will also want to use the

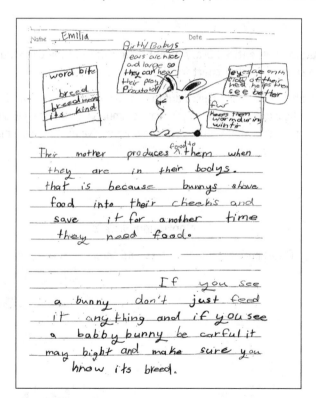

FIG. 2–2   Emilia uses a diagram as well as a key-word box in her piece about how bunnies are born.

Standing in the midst of the writing workshop, I said, "Writers, give me your eyes." Once I had their attention, I continued. "I'm learning so much from *your* books—specifically the things you're *doing* in your books. You know what is cool about that? It means that each of you can get ideas for your own writing not just by studying published authors, but also by studying each other's books! Right now, make a pretend library display of *your* books—just lay them out beautifully. Before you dig in, just admire the display of nonfiction books that your table has produced.

"Now, you have three minutes—just three minutes—to work with your partner to open the book of someone else at your table. Here's the thing—I've given you purple Post-its. Will you place a Post-it where you see that writer doing something and you think, 'Whoa, I could try that!'?"

After the allotted three minutes, I said, "Okay, time's up, writers. I know you have some cool new ideas for your own books. There are purple Post-its everywhere! Be sure to make time to try those things out. Remember, whenever you want to learn something new as a writer, you can study published authors *and* peer authors!"

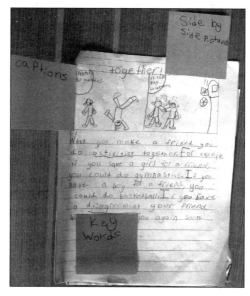

FIG. 2–3   A writer uses Post-its to mark moves in a fellow writer's piece that he wants to try in his own writing.

drawings to mobilize more writing. You might say, "When writers use lots of details to illustrate, it's usually because they are also planning to write with lots of details. Think about how you can teach all of that information in your text. Then pick up your pencil again, and this time, start writing!"

Help writers progress from writing one book to writing another.

Be on the lookout for students who have finished their first book and are ready to start another. You might gather a group of such writers together and say, "Writers, I noticed you seem ready to try out a new topic, which is great! Writers teach about many topics. Think about another topic that you know a lot about already." Give them a minute to think, and ask for a signal when they have an idea. If kids take a while, you can scaffold this by saying things like, "Perhaps you are thinking of a sport you know a lot about. Maybe you know a lot about a place—perhaps a place you go to often . . ." Expect, however, that most kids will have thought of a topic within a minute. You might then invite kids to teach each other about their topics for a few minutes. As you listen to kids talking about topics, grab booklets, help writers make a little plan, and then get them writing. "You can do this whenever one topic runs out and you're ready to write about a new one. It's as easy as that!"

Using Tiny Topics Notepads to Capture Ideas for Nonfiction Books

Alert writers to the fact that they will be writing lots of nonfiction books and will therefore need several topics.

"Nonfiction authors, yesterday you thought of a topic you knew a ton about, grabbed a booklet, and got started writing. You are probably going to need to get ready to write another book soon, and so I thought we could talk about how writers come up with enough ideas for nonfiction books that they can write lots and lots of those books."

Share a strategy for generating topics—in this case, letting the environment, or the world around you, spark possible ideas. Give writers an opportunity to practice.

"The tip I want to give you is that writers think about topics for writing not just when they are in a writing workshop, but all the time. A writer might be at the grocery store, looking at all the kinds of cereals, and think, 'Whoa! I have eaten about ten different kinds of sugary cereals. I could write a whole book called *Tasty Cereals*.' When writers think of a topic, they write it down. Some writers do what you learned to do last unit and that is to carry little notepads with them so they always have a place to record their ideas for topics they could write about.

"So right now, get your Tiny Topics notepad out of your folder. I know it's been lying there, unused for a few days. Get it out, and try keeping it out of your folder and in your pocket, so any day, any time, you can jot ideas for nonfiction books you could write.

"Let's practice. Think of your favorite room at home. In your mind, look around the room and let what you see spark an idea for a nonfiction book you could write. Now—quickly—whip open your notepad and record that idea, fast and furious."

I gave the kids a few seconds, and then said, "Now, look around our classroom and think, 'What reminds me of things I know about?' No talking—just think. Think of two things if you can, maybe three." I left a pool of silence, then I said, "So, writers, now that you have ideas for what you might write about, what do you do?"

A kid whipped open his notepad, and I nodded vigorously, pointing, as if to say, "You've got it."

Then I said, "You can even get ideas for what you could write about from hearing each other's ideas—so do some sharing and see if you can collect even more topics."

It is helpful to channel students to think of topics they are experts on all of the time, not just during writing workshop! Throughout the entire school day, your children do things, use things, and interact with people that they are experts on. For students having an especially hard time generating ideas, pointing this out and having kids write these topics down is useful.

After kids talked and shared for a few minutes, with me cajoling them to let each other's topics spark ideas, I said, "After this, for the whole of your life, always remember that writers live differently than nonwriters. Writers are always going through life thinking, 'I could write a book about *that*.'"

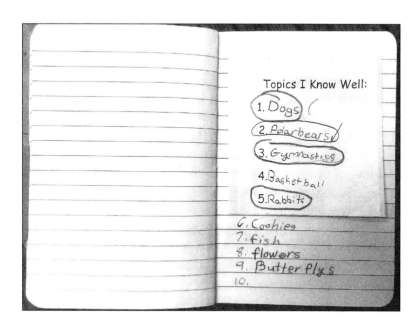

Topics I Know Well:
1. Dogs
2. Polarbears
3. Gymnastics
4. Basketball
5. Rabbits
6. Cookies
7. fish
8. flowers
9. Butterflys
10.

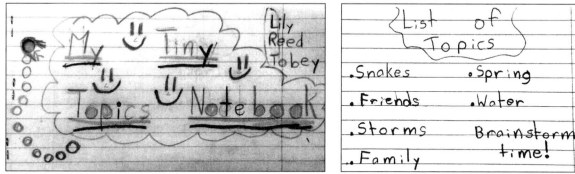

FIG. 2–4   Writers record their ideas for future nonfiction books in their Tiny Topics notepads.

Nonfiction Writers
Squeeze Their Brains

Writing Long to Teach Readers a Lot of Information

IN THIS SESSION, you'll teach children that nonfiction writers can write more on each page. They do this by rereading and then thinking, "What else could I say?"

GETTING READY

✔ Your demonstration book, written in a bare-bones manner so that students can practice elaboration (see Connection and Link)

✔ "Nonfiction Writers" anchor chart (see Link)

✔ Student writing folders containing the books they are writing (see Active Engagement)

✔ Scissors, tape, and revision strips (see Mid-Workshop Teaching)

✔ Single sheets of writing paper in the writing center (see Share)

LOOK AT A STACK OF WRITING produced by second-graders, and the first thing that you'll notice is that the writing tends to be underdeveloped. Mina Shaughnessy, the great writing researcher who wrote *Errors and Expectations*, points out that the writing of basic writers in community colleges often tends to suffer the same problem. Inexperienced writers tend to write in "sentences of thought" rather than "paragraphs of thought." You may find that you tend to do this as well. Right now, in your mind, pretend you are writing about your kids' nonfiction writing. Just write your observations of their writing.

Perhaps you wrote, "Second-graders' writing is often hard to read because of the spelling problems. It can also be pretty short." Right there, in that instance, you would be writing in sentences of thought: one sentence about the spelling, one about the length. You'd be well advised to keep the mantra "say more" in mind. This time, the text might go: "Second-graders' writing is often hard to read because of the spelling problems. There are quite a few second-graders who still spell phonetically, which means the reader has to work out what the words are saying. Sometimes the kids who spell poorly also write in teeny-tiny letters, almost as if they don't want someone to read their writing." That's writing in a paragraph, not a sentence, of thought. Do you see the importance of that mantra: *say more*?

Today's session gives students a really simple, fundamental message: say more. That advice is good for the writer as he or she writes, and it is also good as a go-to revision strategy. Once the advice is linked to revision, it becomes, "Reread, think 'What else could I say?' and figure out how and where to insert more information." That's the lesson for today.

In today's mid-workshop, you may want to teach your students how to insert that information into their texts. You could, of course, decide to tuck that tip into the actual minilesson, leaving yourself free to teach whatever arises as your kids work.

But a word to the wise: the conferring and small-group write-up for today is particularly important because in the end, the one thing that does the most to encourage writers to say more is the presence of a listener who listens with rapt interest. During your conferring and small-group time, you need to be that listener, and equally importantly, you need to set kids up to be that listener for each other.

Nonfiction Writers Squeeze Their Brains
Writing Long to Teach Readers a Lot of Information

CONNECTION

Ask children to give you their feedback on a bare-bones book you tell across your fingers, prompting them to notice that it lacks information.

"Writers, tell me what you'd think of this book." I began talking through a bare-bones book, touching as I read it aloud.

> Page 1: Breakfast is in the morning.
> Page 2: Some people eat cereal.
> Page 3: Some people skip breakfast.

"So what do you think? Wasn't my book the *greatest*? Did you learn a *ton* about breakfast?!"

Kids shook their heads.

"No?! What? What was the problem?"

"It didn't have enough information," Morgan offered.

Based on children's feedback, suggest that you should squeeze your brain to come up with something else to add to the book.

"Ohhh! I should say more. Like . . . after I write one thing, I should squeeze my brain and try to come up with one *more* thing to say? Hmm, . . . let me try it." Returning to the same bare-bones book, I touched a page and tried again: "'Breakfast is in the morning.' Let me squeeze my brain." I pressed my fingers to my temples to demonstrate this. "Let me think of one more thing. Oh! I know. 'Many people eat breakfast with their families and use that talking time to get excited about their day.'"

Notice we turn to a concrete image—squeezing your brain—to convey to children what it means to think really hard—in this case, so as to put all the information they know onto the page. "Squeezing your brain!" It's a bit graphic, even perhaps gross, but it is an image that threads through many of the Units of Study books and your kids will know well what it means. If you make a gesture to show what you mean by squeezing your brain, you'll be able in the future to simply add that gesture as a rallying cry for kids to think hard.

Name the teaching point.

"Today I want to teach you that nonfiction writers know their readers want all the information the author can give them. That means nonfiction writers go from writing to rereading what they've written, and when they reread, they squeeze their brains to think up more information to add to their writing."

TEACHING

Recruit one child to read aloud the first chapter of his information book. Then ask him to squeeze his brain to think of more information he could add to that page.

"Raymond, bring your book about baseball up here." Raymond scrambled forward. "Raymond, could you turn to your first chapter and read it to us?" He opened up his booklet and read:

Baseball Teams
You play on teams. The baseball team has to work *together*.

"So, writers, will you join me in thinking about a tip we could give Raymond? Now that he has written that interesting chapter, what might he do next?" I asked. The kids chimed in that Raymond could reread and try to say more.

I nodded, making a squeezing motion with my hands, and gestured for Raymond to take over.

"Hmm," Raymond said, "I know that different teams have names like the Mets and the Yankees."

"And all the people on the team wear the same color!" Lily chimed in.

Debrief in a way that makes the work transferable to other days, other students, other texts.

I nodded. "So, class, do you think if Raymond reread his chapter and squeezed his brain, he could think of more information to add?" The class joined me in nodding. "And do the rest of you think you could do similar work today and often after you have written a chapter?" The class concurred.

"Writers, remember that first Raymond reread what he already wrote, and then he squeezed his brain for more information to add to his chapter. Now, he has enough information to write long—all the way down the page!" I held up Raymond's chapter, pointing down the lines.

Nonfiction writers will often teach an important point about their subject at the beginning of a chapter and then spend the rest of the chapter expounding on that point. They might do this by giving examples, defining important terms, teaching how something works or why it happens, or even describing their point in ...

TP: Readers (Bring Fillers) want all the information the author can give them

★ Pull someone up... how could you squeeze your brain

ACTIVE ENGAGEMENT

Channel one partner to reread his or her chapter and to tell the other things that could be added to the chapter.

"It's your turn. When you're ready, Partner 1, will you reread one of your chapters, and tell Partner 2 things you could add to it? Partner 2s, you might be able to help your partner think of even more information to add to the page."

As partners started to share, I called out some little coaching tips: "If you've thought of one thing to add, think of another!" "If you are stuck and can't think of more to add, try rereading the chapter." "Try asking yourself questions, like 'Can I give an example?' or 'Can I tell a lot more about one particular part?'"

LINK

Ask students to share tips for how you can improve your demonstration text.

"Writers, do you remember the word *elaboration*? You saw that word earlier this year, on your narrative checklist. And the important thing for you to know is that elaboration—or telling more—is a really big deal for all writers, whether you are writing stories or all-about books or really, almost anything. So will you and your partner think again about the book I shared with you at the start of today's minilesson, and see if you have specific tips for how I can improve this book?" I showed my book that went like this:

> Page 1: Breakfast is in the morning. Many people eat breakfast with their families and use that talking time to get excited about their day.
> Page 2: Some people eat cereal.
> Page 3: Some people skip breakfast.

"You'll remember that you did *not* think my book was the greatest. Why? Because you didn't learn a *ton* about breakfast! But now you all have a strategy for helping to fix that. After you write a page, you reread and add more. I can tell that you are eager to get writing. Some of you are still finishing your first book, and all of you have topics from yesterday for new books—so either finish one book up and then start a new one, or go right to the new book. Ready? Set? Go!"

ANCHOR CHART

Nonfiction Writers

- Read books by other writers and think "I could try that!"
- **Reread their early drafts, trying to add more.**

Note that within a ten-minute minilesson, you probably do not have time for the partners to switch roles, and that is not generally advised. In this instance, the partner who talks about his or her writing will benefit—but so, too, will the listener. And the whole point of this lesson is that it is transferable, so it certainly should apply to Partner 2's book even if he or she doesn't discuss that book now.

Reread their early drafts, trying to add more

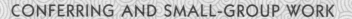

Supporting Students to Move Forward as Nonfiction Writers

Use conversation to support writers as they grow information around a topic.

As you prepare to confer and lead small groups today, it will help if you take a moment to anticipate a few of the predictable things you'll be likely to do today. You are going to want to be an intent listener, conveying through your rapt interest that you are dying to learn what your youngsters have to teach.

Practice simply reading kids' work as if it is gold. Read a bit with absolute interest, then pause, repeat what you have learned, and let it sink in. If the child writes, "Toy bulldogs have to drink from a special bowl or they will die," put that page down and be astounded. "Really? How did that dog live in the wild? What is that special bowl like and how does it keep them from *dying*? This is amazing."

My point is not about bulldogs, but instead about listening. Try to actually be fascinated with the topics that your students address in little books. They will sense your energy and be inspired by it. Of course, these deeper conversations will teach kids to think more deeply and encourage them to unearth content that is sure to interest readers. Above all, these conversations can serve as models for the conversations that you will want to set kids up to have with each other.

Pull a small group of writers who need support moving from stagnation to productivity.

There is one more, smaller but also important point to bring up. Whenever we teach one thing, some kids will overdo it. You teach exclamation marks, and some kids start using whole swaths of them: big bold exclamations for the truly big events, lines full of exclamations for things that are really exciting. Similarly, you can expect that after you teach kids to reread a page, squeezing their minds to say more, some kids will become so committed to that work that they don't balance that work with the need to move on. If the writer pauses to think, "Do I have more to say?," gives a bit of time for more information to surface and then nothing does surface, the writer needs to turn the page and start a new chapter or a new book. That is particularly important now, at the start of this unit. One of your biggest goals is to set kids up to write up a storm, cranking out book after book without feeling duty bound to wait for your approval before progressing to another book or another topic.

You might, therefore, gather a group of kids together who seem to be lingering overly long on a single chapter. "Writers, can I stop you for just a moment? I notice some of you seem to have gotten stuck. Sometimes this happens, writers. You try to squeeze your brain for more and more information, but no luck." The kids in the group will concur and you'll continue by saying, "Writers, what you need to know is that that's okay. Sometimes your brain has nothing left for a certain chapter. The worst thing you can do is let that stop you from writing *a lot*! So if you get stuck on one chapter, don't freeze. Just turn to the next chapter and start there. And guess what? You can always come back to that earlier chapter at a later time. So for now, don't let anything stop you from keeping your pens moving down the page!"

Standing in the midst of the room, I asked for students' attention. "Writers, I'm totally impressed that you aren't just adding more at the bottom of your page, but you are instead figuring out *where* to add more. Like if I wanted to add that Fruit Loops® are one of the most popular cereals in the whole wide world, would I put that at the *end* of my page?" I said, then reread the page aloud:

> Some people eat cereal. Some eat pancakes.

The kids all agreed that no, it would be silly to write, "Some people eat cereal. Some eat pancakes. Fruit Loops are the most popular cereal in the world." "So, writers, will you show each other ways that you have invented to stick the information into the right place on your page?"

The room became a hubbub of chatter. After a bit, I interrupted. "Writers, eyes up here," I said and waited for their attention. I held up Lily's book. "When Lily wanted to add more, she used a strip of paper that she stuck off the edge of her page to fit the information into the right place. You can all try that—get scissors and tape and use those tools to help you add on. Or you could do like Brian and draw arrows that show where exactly the information goes.

"So get back to it, writers. Don't let anything stop you from keeping your pens moving down the page!"

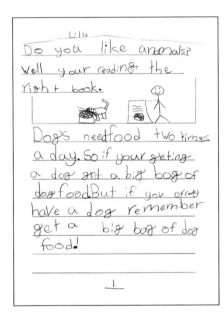

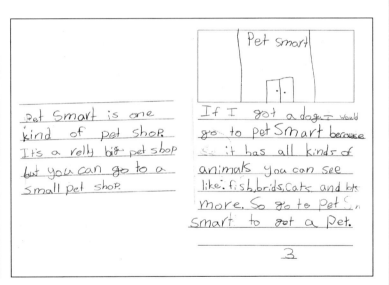

FIG. 3–1   Lily used flaps to revise the pages of her book to teach more.

Adding onto Chapters, Making Them More Than One Page

Draw attention to writers who used arrows and strips of paper to add information to chapters. Show writers that they can also add a new page to a chapter.

"Writers, as you wrung out your brains, adding even more information to each chapter, your writing was even longer than you expected! I noticed the coolest thing—the length of the paper didn't stop you from adding more and more information. Many of you used arrows and strips of paper to say even more."

I held up Stella's book. "Stella did something different. When she had written all the way down her page, she knew she had a lot more to say. She didn't just say, 'Oh, well, I guess that's it for this chapter!' No way! She went and got a whole new page from the writing center and added it into her book. That made her chapter *two* pages long!" I flipped back and forth so the class could see the length of Stella's chapter.

Reveal that when students are writing long, sometimes information ends up in the wrong place. To fix that, they can reread.

"Writers, I bet many of you are ready to add more to your chapters if you've run out of space, but remember, it's going to be important to reread after squeezing out your brain to make sure that all of your information ends up in the right place. Sometimes, when we are trying to write more and more, we write things that don't fit in the chapter.

"You can all try out Stella's strategy of not just adding one strip, but a whole new page if you feel like you have a lot more information to give in one chapter. Then, reread thinking about whether the information all fits. If it doesn't, no big deal! Get some scissors, cut it out, and tape it right where it belongs."

As writers exercise their nonfiction writing muscles, you will soon see them produce pages of writing instead of simply lines of writing.

The paper choice and revision tools you offer writers set an expectation for the amount of writing they can produce. If you notice students writing down the page and then squishing a last sentence in at the bottom, use that as a signal that they need paper choice with more lines or extra paper in their folders or in the middle of their table.

Session 4

Writers Set Goals and Make Plans

THE SIMPLE ACT of children noticing and naming the work they have done pays off in a number of important ways. Doing this makes their work more memorable and replicable and gives children vocabulary for talking and thinking about their own writing. You will not want to wait until the end of a unit to teach children to look back over their writing again and again.

At this point, your children will have written two, perhaps three, very quick nonfiction books. Each book will contain a few chapters and perhaps some features they noticed as they studied a mentor text. This is a perfect time for writers to turn their attention to the work that lies ahead. In second grade, some of the biggest shifts come in the areas of development. If you place the first- and second-grade checklists side by side, you will notice that in the area of development, first-graders are expected to put facts in their writing, but by second grade the expectation is that writers will use different kinds of information (facts, definitions, details, steps, and tips), as well as include words that show expertise about a topic. The books your children have written so far are apt to reflect expectations from first grade, therefore becoming aware of the new expectations will serve your kids well.

In this session, you will offer both the first-grade and second-grade checklists to writers, but you will guide students through the items on the second-grade checklist. The checklist details end-of-grade expectations, so your kids will probably not have accomplished this work already—but some precocious writers may be able to check *yes* for a few items on the second-grade checklist. To make sure that kids actually have evidence that they've done something repeatedly before they regard an expectation as met, encourage them to hold one of the books they have written alongside the checklist, using Post-its to mark each place where the writer has accomplished something. Of course, marginal dots work as well as Post-its and are cheaper!

Then later in this session, you will teach your youngsters that writers set goals and make plans for those goals. You can expect that all of your writers will leave today with goals and plans.

IN THIS SESSION, you'll teach children that writers get stronger by looking at their writing, setting goals, and making plans.

GETTING READY

✔ By the beginning of this session, students should have written at least two books. If you have students who have not met this target, you may wish to devote some time during the conferring and small-group work to supporting their efforts to increase volume.

✔ Students' writing folders with Post-its and pens inside (see Teaching)

✔ Photos of one or two professional writers' writing spaces (see Connection)

✔ Copies of the Information Writing Checklist, grades 1 and 2, for each student, plus one to display to the class (see Teaching)

✔ "Nonfiction Writers" anchor chart (see Link)

Writers Set Goals and Make Plans

CONNECTION

Congratulate children on the success they are having as nonfiction authors. Then share with them the research you did of professional writers' walls, pointing out the inspirational goal quotations.

"Writers you are on your way to becoming successful nonfiction authors. You're writing books to fill the library, learning from mentor authors, and teaching up a storm!

"But, just to be sure that you're doing it up like the pros, I went ahead and did a little research." I put a picture or two of a couple of writers' workspaces up for kids to see.

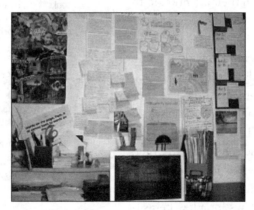

"Take a look at these professional writers' work spaces. Do you see what I see? There are the things you'd expect—books and writing materials and a desk—but there's something else, too. Do you see the walls? These writers have things tacked up on their walls—bits of writing.

"Of course I became curious. I wondered, 'What do all those things say?' So I investigated. After a little more research I discovered that writers have quotes like these hanging up on their walls:

> 'A goal without a plan is just a wish.'

> 'Set a goal. Tell the world.'

C: Celebrate
successes

- Writers are always
growing

"Are you realizing what I realized? These writers know about *goals*. I bet they have things they are working toward in their own writing. Those quotes are hanging up to remind them of that."

❖ **Name the teaching point.**

"Whenever someone wants to get good at something, wants to improve, they practice. Today, I want to teach you that writers are no different. They work hard to improve their writing by setting goals and then making plans to work toward those goals."

TEACHING

Set writers up to evaluate their writing by introducing the Information Writing Checklist for first and second grades.

"In your last unit you used a tool called the Narrative Writing Checklist to set goals to make your stories better. Now that you're writing nonfiction, though, you need a slightly different tool." I pulled out the Information Writing Checklist for grades 1 and 2 and placed it under the document camera so that children could see it. "I'm going to show you both the first-grade goals and the second-grade goals, but we will focus on using the second-grade goals today.

"Let's take a quick tour of the second-grade side of the checklist. You'll see the same headings as the ones on the narrative checklist—the items listed under Structure all pertain to ways your nonfiction book is organized. The items listed

You can place the checklist under a document camera if you have one, but it is fine if you also just read it out loud. You can place copies of the checklist on each table after the minilesson. If your students are unfamiliar with checklists and have not previously been taught from the Units of Study in Opinion, Information, and Narrative Writing series, you might take a few moments to teach them how to use a checklist to self-assess their writing. For more information about using checklists, you may wish to read Chapter 5, "Introducing Students to the Self-Assessment Checklists," in Writing Pathways, *Grades K–5.*

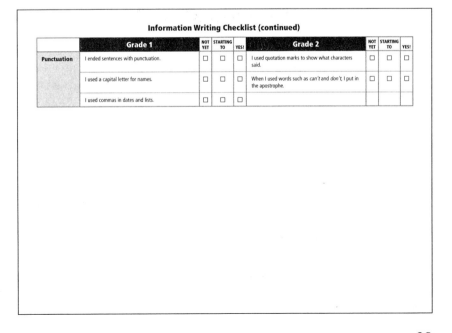

Name: _____   Date: _____

Information Writing Checklist

	Grade 1	NOT YET	STARTING TO	YES!	Grade 2	NOT YET	STARTING TO	YES!
	Structure				**Structure**			
Overall	I taught my readers about a topic.	☐	☐	☐	I taught readers some important points about a subject.	☐	☐	☐
Lead	I named my topic in the beginning and got my readers' attention.	☐	☐	☐	I wrote a beginning in which I named a subject and tried to interest readers.	☐	☐	☐
Transitions	I told different parts about my topic on different pages.	☐	☐	☐	I used words such as *and* and *also* to show I had more to say.	☐	☐	☐
Ending	I wrote an ending.	☐	☐	☐	I wrote some sentences or a section at the end to wrap up my piece.	☐	☐	☐
Organization	I told about my topic part by part.	☐	☐	☐	My writing had different parts. Each part told different information about the topic.	☐	☐	☐
	Development				**Development**			
Elaboration	I put facts in my writing to teach about my topic.	☐	☐	☐	I used different kinds of information in my writing such as facts, definitions, details, steps, and tips	☐	☐	☐
Craft	I used labels and words to give facts.	☐	☐	☐	I tried to include the words that showed I'm an expert on the topic.	☐	☐	☐
	Language Conventions				**Language Conventions**			
Spelling	I used all I knew about words and chunks (*at, op, it,* etc.) to help me spell.	☐	☐	☐	I used what I knew about spelling patterns (*tion, er, ly,* etc.) to spell a word.	☐	☐	☐
	I spelled the word wall words right and used the word wall to help me spell other words.	☐	☐	☐	I spelled all of the word wall words correctly and used the word wall to help me figure out how to spell other words.	☐	☐	☐

Information Writing Checklist (continued)

	Grade 1	NOT YET	STARTING TO	YES!	Grade 2	NOT YET	STARTING TO	YES!
Punctuation	I ended sentences with punctuation.	☐	☐	☐	I used quotation marks to show what characters said.	☐	☐	☐
	I used a capital letter for names.	☐	☐	☐	When I used words such as *can't* and *don't,* I put in the apostrophe.	☐	☐	☐
	I used commas in dates and lists.	☐	☐	☐				

under Development all pertain to ways you say more, or elaborate. The items listed under Language Conventions are things you can do to make your writing easier for others to read.

"Of course, you have just started your work this year as nonfiction writers, so there will be things that you're not yet doing and things that you do only sometimes. These can become your goals!"

Scaffold students' self-evaluation by reading aloud items from the secondary checklist and adding in clarifying tips. Ask writers to mark their own pieces when they find evidence of accomplishing an item.

"So, writers, put one of your nonfiction books in front of you, and choose one where you have done a lot of work. Then take out the stack of Post-its I've put in your writing folder. As I read through the items on the second-grade side of the checklist, look for evidence of that work in your book. When you find evidence in your writing, leave a Post-it to mark that evidence. Be tough on yourself, and don't say something is evidence if really, you haven't yet done that thing on the checklist."

I read the first item of the grade 2 side of the checklist, "I taught readers some important points about a subject," and then tucked in some clarification. "Teaching important points about a subject could look like a table of contents for your topic, or it could be that you used headings across your chapters to signal to your reader the bigger points addressed in your book. If you've done this work, leave a Post-it to mark it." I continued reading down the checklist, giving quick tips and clarifying certain items.

Acknowledge that writers often find criteria they have not yet met; these items become goals. Then quickly reread the checklist, inviting children to listen for items they can mark as their own goals.

"Writers, you are already doing so many important things as nonfiction writers. I see pages and parts marked across your books.

"I am certain, though, there were a few items you weren't yet able to mark—items you couldn't find evidence for. I am also certain there were items where you said, 'Sort of . . .' because you did it a little bit, but not really. Am I right, writers?"

Heads nodded across the rug.

"I love seeing some of you nodding your heads, realizing that what you have done isn't really at the second-grade level yet. That is brave, smart work—thinking, 'I'm not yet done with that job.' Good going. The fact is, all of these items," I gestured toward the checklist, "are goals for you to reach by the *end* of second grade. So it will be great to find things you haven't yet done—they become your goals. It seems like you're ready for your very own checklist. I passed copies of the checklist out to the class.

"I'm going to read through the items one more time. As I read, look back at your book, your Post-its, and think, 'What have I only sort of done, what things on this checklist could I do a *lot* more and a *lot* better? Those items can become your goals, and it will be by having a lot of goals that you make your writing get better and better."

Part of the work of using tools, such as check-lists, and setting goals involves understanding the criteria. While your children may have used the first-grade side of the Information Writing Checklist last year during the Nonfiction Chapter Books unit, the criteria will change somewhat from first grade to second grade. You can use this part of the minilesson to emphasize areas in which a significant shift has occurred.

Give children a moment between items of the checklist to scan their book, but do not wait until every child is done before moving on to the next item. The idea is exposure more than perfection. There will be other opportunities across the unit for writers to become more proficient in noticing the criteria and engaging in self-assessment.

You will want to play up the work of reflecting to determine goals as important work. You can use this as an opportunity to support a growth mind-set—that there will always be ways to improve.

After leaving kids a minute to do this work, I added, "Turn and talk to your partner about the items you are taking as goals—and consider making some fireworks or stars beside those goals, because they're going to be the best thing in the world for you."

	Grade 1	NOT YET	STARTING TO	YES!	Grade 2	NOT YET	STARTING TO	YES!
	Structure				**Structure**			
Overall	I taught my readers about a topic.	☐	☐	☐	I taught readers some important points about a subject.	☐	☐	☐
Lead	I named my topic in the beginning and got my readers' attention.	☐	☐	☐	I wrote a beginning in which I named a subject and tried to interest readers.	☐	☐	☐
Transitions	I told different parts about my topic on different pages.	☐	☐	☐	I used words such as *and* and *also* to show I had more to say.	☐	☐	☐
Ending	I wrote an ending.	☐	☐	☐	I wrote some sentences or a section at the end to wrap up my piece.	☐	☐	☐
Organization	I told about my topic part by part.	☐	☐	☐	My writing had different parts. Each part told different information about the topic.	☐	☐	☐
	Development				**Development**			
Elaboration	I put facts in my writing to teach about my topic.	☐	☐	☐	I used different kinds of information in my writing such as facts, definitions, details, steps, and tips	☐	☐	☐
Craft	I used labels and words to give facts.	☐	☐	☐	I tried to include the words that showed I'm an expert on the topic.	☐	☐	☐
	Language Conventions				**Language Conventions**			
Spelling	I used all I knew about words and chunks (*at, op, it,* etc.) to help me spell.	☐	☐	☐	I used what I knew about spelling patterns (*tion, er, ly,* etc.) to spell a word.	☐	☐	☐
	I spelled the word wall words right and used the word wall to help me spell other words.	☐	☐	☐	I spelled all of the word wall words correctly and used the word wall to help me figure out how to spell other words.	☐	☐	☐

Name: _____ Date: _____

Information Writing Checklist

FIG. 4–1   A student uses fireworks to mark goals on the Information Writing Checklist.

ACTIVE ENGAGEMENT

Invite a few writers to share their goals as a way to make goal-setting public.

"Writers, that was some important work you just did—setting goals. I'd like some of you to be brave and share your goals out loud. Everyone, let's listen closely. You will most likely find that someone else shares your goals!"

Morgan began, "I wrote about Legos® but I forgot to end my piece. I just had a last page." Other writers nodded as well; they need to work on their endings, too. "Let's hear another goal."

"I wrote *a lot* about dogs," Lily said. "It was just a lot of facts. I didn't have the other kinds like the checklist said."

"Ah, yes, in second grade we need to push ourselves to include different kinds of information. I bet many of you set that as your goal." Kids nodded in agreement.

Making goals public makes you more likely to accomplish them. Once others know what you are working toward, they can offer more specific feedback and support.

Highlight that to really strengthen their writing, writers need to make plans to go along with their goals, and invite kids to do the same.

"Lily and Morgan just took a big first step. They named a goal. I am sure they have a few others, too! Here's the deal—there are actually two big steps to goal-setting." Eyes widened. "I know! Two big steps, but they are both super important and will help you become the best writer you can be.

"The second big step is to take your goals and make plans. Remember, a goal without a plan is just a wish!" I brought back a quote from the connection to drive home my point.

"Let's all give this a try. Right now, put a goal or two of yours in your mind. Point to them on the checklist if you have to. Now make a plan. Think about what will help you accomplish those goals. What will you do today to work toward those goals? Give me a thumbs up when you're ready.

"Are you ready to take two big steps, writers? Turn and share your goal *and* your plan with your partner."

After listening in for a few moments I called everyone back. "Writers, what you've done right now is really important work. Now that you've named goals and plans you can begin working toward, your books are going to get even better!"

LINK

Send students off to write, emphasizing that writers carry their goals with them as they write. Add the final point to the anchor chart for this bend.

"Writers, just like you do every day, you will work on your nonfiction books, but today is a little different. Today you have goals to help you along. You also made plans. Hold these goals and plans in your mind as you write—they can help you revise books you've already written as well as start new ones.

ANCHOR CHART

Nonfiction Writers

- Read books by other writers and think "I could try that!"
- Reread their early drafts, trying to add more.
- **Set goals and make plans.**

Today you are supporting writers as they self-assess and provide feedback for themselves. John Hattie states in Visible Learning *that there are three questions involved in feedback: Where am I going?, How am I going there?, and Where to next? Today, students are working to answer all three. They have the criteria of the checklist to help them clarify where they're going. Using the checklist to assess their writing helps students answer to how they are moving toward the criteria. Then by stating clear goals, items not yet practiced, and by making plans, they have an answer to what's next.*

Working toward Goals Requires Revision

Take a moment to notice how students settle into the work of using goals and plans as they write.

By the time students go off to write today, they will have a handful of goals and some tentative plans for meeting those goals. You will want to take a moment to observe how they tackle the work of using their goals to revise their books. Undoubtedly there will be a variety of interpretations of this work. Many students will remember the work they did in narrative writing and will reach for some revision strips or perhaps a new page or two. Other students will have been less ambitious in their self-assessment and will seem content adding a sprinkling of words here and there. A handful of students may even just carry on with the work they already had in mind from the day before—oblivious to your invitation for them to revise.

Lift the level of work through table conferences.

It may be wise to begin this part of the workshop with some quick table conferences to get all writers into the spirit of working toward ambitious goals and large-scale revision. When you approach a table, take a moment to assess where students are in their understanding of this work so that you can decide on a tip that will benefit all the writers present.

A typical scenario is for you to note that your writers are engaging in only very small-scale revisions. You might say, "Writers, I was just watching you work toward your goals. One thing I noticed is that many of you are trying to take a really *big* goal like transitions or teaching with a variety of information, and yet you are working on that goal in teeny tiny ways. You're trying to squish those big goals into a few words, added into the margins of a chapter you have already written. Can I give you a tip? When writers have big goals, like all of you do, they work on those goals in big ways. They often need to work on a *whole new page* so they can try a chapter or a part of a book all over again—this time working to accomplish that goal as they write."

You might press for writers to do that. "Right now, put your finger on an important revision you made." If you wait for a moment, the children will do this. "Is this revision a small one (like a line or two) or a big one (like a page or two)?" If you listen in, you'll hear students agree that their revision was a small one. That's great for them to see—and now they can set to the job of making more large-scale improvements.

(continues)

> ## MID-WORKSHOP TEACHING
> ### Writers Can Bring Goals from Book to Book
>
> "Writers, I am sure you know this, but I just wanted to remind you about the cool thing about goals. Goals don't just belong to one book. They belong to all of your books. Goals can move from book to book."
>
> I picked up Sasha's book and noticed one of her goals was to name her topic and get readers interested. "Check this out, writers. So Sasha, I have a huge question to ask you. Your goal was to get your readers interested in your topic. Did you think of this goal, as a goal just for your kitten book, or did you take this goal and use it on another book?"
>
> Sasha screwed her face up a bit as she thought and then pointed to the kitten book. Nodding, I said, "So you used that goal of getting people interested to write a great hook at the start of *Kittens*, right?" She nodded. "Sasha—and all of you—what do you think would be the super-smart thing to do next?"
>
> This time there was general consensus that the smart thing would be for Sasha to take the goal of getting readers interested, and to try using that goal to improve other books she'd written.

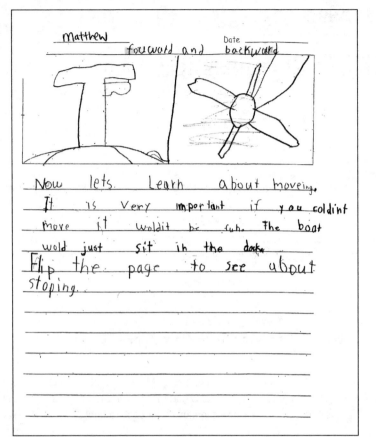

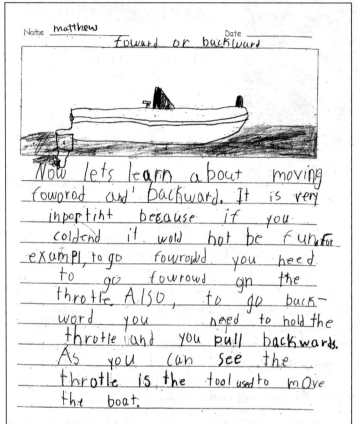

FIG. 4–2   Matthew's first draft of his chapter about driving a boat and then his revised draft after using the checklist and being prompted toward large-scale revision during a table conference.

Help writers revise their mindset around goals.

Some students will have been more reluctant right from the start in setting goals for themselves. It will be important for you to approach these writers with the idea of supporting their mind-set around goals. You might look at their book topic and use that to generate a quick example around goal-setting and growth. If the writer's topic is dancing, for example, you could say, "Dancers work to improve their dancing all the time. They study elite dancers, learn new combinations of moves, and practice for hours on end—they have goals and plans!" Then you can invite the child to take on this same work for themselves as a writer.

You could also approach writers who are reluctant to revisit their work by reminding them of all the ways they have grown, as a person and as a writer, from the beginning of the year until now. You could say, "Every week I am seeing you grow. At the beginning of the year you needed reminders to keep going with your writing and now you can write for twenty-five minutes at a time without stopping! You have changed so much. So I know you're ready to change in other ways as a writer, too."

Goal-setting and revision are not just about writing pieces becoming stronger, but about the writers themselves growing and changing.

Writers Rehearse "About the Author" Pages

Invite writers to rehearse ideas for an "about the author" page by interviewing each other.

"Writers, a few days ago I introduced you to some nonfiction authors from our classroom library—Seymour Simon and Gail Gibbons. You didn't *actually* meet them, but you got to know them. You learned their favorite topics, how many books they've written, even how they get their ideas when you listened to me read aloud their 'about the author' pages.

"Authors write these pages so that readers can learn who they are and how they work. That gave me an idea. I thought you might want to write 'about the author' pages, too! What do you think? Are you game?" Kids nodded eagerly.

"Great! In a minute, Partner 1, you'll interview Partner 2 to rehearse ideas for an 'about the author' page. Partner 1, you might ask questions like, 'What are some of your favorite topics to write about?' or 'Where do you ideas come from?' I bet you'll come up with a *lot* more questions. Partner 1, act as interviewer and ask the questions." I held my hand up like I was holding a microphone. "Partner 2, get ready to share information about yourself as a nonfiction author."

As partners interviewed each other, I listened for fruitful questions kids were asking that I could voice over to the class. "Stella just asked her partner *where* she does her best writing. Readers would love to know that little tidbit of information. Sasha wanted to know *how* her partner gets all the information for his books. Maybe you'll want to ask your partner that, also!"

After two minutes I asked, "Authors, do you think you have enough bits of information to write your 'about the author' page?" The class gave me a big thumbs up. "I know readers will love to learn not only about your topic but also about *you*! So, during writing workshop tomorrow, you might choose to create an 'about the author' page."

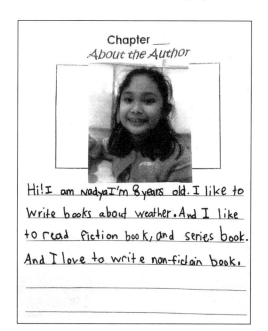

FIG. 4–3 Nadya's "about the author" page where she shares information about herself as a writer.

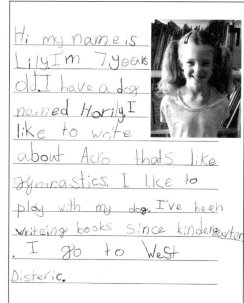

FIG. 4–4 Lily's "about the author" page where she shares information about her favorite activities.

A Trip to the Editor

Preparing for a "Meet the Author" Celebration

Dear Teachers,

If you have been teaching with support from the Units of Study in Opinion, Information, and Narrative Writing series, you will be accustomed to occasionally finding that instead of writing a minilesson out in great detail, we sometimes write you a letter and help you to plan the details of a session. This is one of those letters. The letter aims to hand the reins of the session over to you. Whenever letters appear instead of full sessions in these books, this is a signal that we hope you plan your own minilesson, conferences, and small-group work, and will help you do so, following the lead of your students.

It's the final day of the first bend, so chances are good that you'll want to rally your kids to celebrate the work they have done so far! You launched your class into the world of nonfiction writing with the message that nonfiction writing isn't as daunting as it may appear. You will have taught this bend with the goal of getting writers to produce a lot of work quickly, moving through the writing process in just a week's time. By now, your students' folders should be filled with at least two, if not more, books that teach others about topics on which the writer is passionate.

In the previous session, you asked children to use a writing checklist as a tool to revise their work. Revision usually entails substantial changes to a piece of work. It may involve changes to the organization of the piece, such as dividing a lengthy chapter into two or adding an introduction, or changes to how the piece is developed, such as adding to one part of a chapter to teach more. In the share from Session 4, you invited students to add an "about the author" page to each of their books.

Today's minilesson will take your class one step further as they edit and share their pieces. Editing is different from revision in that it allows writers to look closely at their sentences and words and make changes that will affect the readability of the piece. Your writers will already know that writers edit their writing, and today you remind them of that. Specifically, we suggest you put editing front and center and give your children the reminders, tools, and support they need to tackle this detailed work. In your classroom, partners could function as each other's editors, and later kids could take on this role for themselves. Today, you could teach your kids to assume the role of editor, looking at their books with new eyes, asking themselves, "Does my writing make sense, sound right, and look right?"

MINILESSON

You may want to begin your minilesson by reminding students of the revision work they did in the previous session. You might say, "Yesterday you read your book with a checklist in hand. Your checklist helped you to set goals and make plans for revision. Many of you revised your chapters to make sure your information was organized into parts and that you taught not just with facts, but also with steps and tips. This is one kind of work nonfiction writers do when they get ready to publish!" You could then ask students to take out their checklists, point to the goals they set for themselves, and show their partner places where they used the checklist to make their writing even better—or places where they *could* have done that.

Then, suggest to kids that writers usually shift between the more large-scale revisions and more fine-grained edits. You could collect from kids their understanding of the sorts of things writers notice and fix up when they edit.

The kids who remember something about editing will probably talk about checking spelling. You can celebrate that, and add onto it as well. You might mention that during editing, the focus is on making sure that readers will have an easy time reading the text really well. So yes, that means working on spelling, but there is also work to do making sure that words haven't been left out, punctuation hasn't been skipped, and that the sentences sound right. Sometimes, to do that work, a writer edits his or her own work. But sometimes the writer enlists the help of someone who doesn't already know the text, asking "Will you read this while I watch?" and then observing where the reader stumbles or seems confused. The reader can also act as a coeditor, spotting things that the writer didn't notice.

Specifically, your teaching point might say, "Writers, today I want to remind you that when writers reread their writing, they not only check that their piece has great content and is well organized, but they also reread as an editor. They check their spelling, grammar, and punctuation to make their piece easier for their readers to understand."

In the teaching portion of the minilesson, you might invite the class as a whole to be your coeditor, and to join you in reading a portion of your draft, listening for places where punctuation needs to be added or changed and looking for words that are tricky to read and need to be spelled again. If you choose to use your own chapter, be sure you have included errors that mirror the ones your second-graders tend to make.

It could be helpful to give writers a tool to help them remember what they are on the lookout for. You could have them turn to the Language Conventions portion of the Information Writing Checklist or utilize the editing list they came up with in the connection. Feel free to add on a few things you know most writers in your classroom need to listen and look for. A list of possibilities is shown in the "Writers Can Edit For" chart that is also available in the online resources.

During the active engagement, you might channel students to work in partnerships, asking one partner to be the coeditor of another partner's writing. As you coach into their work, you may find reason to emphasize that editors reread writing very carefully—they don't race from one page to the next page. You might also suggest that writers find it helps to read their writing out loud so they can hear when something doesn't make sense or sound right. Or you could say, "Be on the lookout for sentences that go on and on. Those can confuse your reader!" You'll want to remind students of the resources they have around the room to fix words that don't look right.

As you send children off to edit on their own, remind them to take as much care in their own work as they did with their partner's work. You might find little spots across the room for children to sit so that they can read their work aloud, hearing places to edit.

CONFERRING AND SMALL-GROUP WORK

As children work, you may want to check to be sure they are enjoying being vigilant. It will help if you have a repertoire of potential conferences and small groups that you can draw on. For starters, you'll want to watch kids work and to notice when writers seem to think this is a race to be done. There is a famous quote about a writer who said, "I spent this morning adding a comma into my story, and this afternoon, taking it out." That is, for writers, this is not slapdash work, and often before settling on one way that a sentence could go, a writer tries a whole bunch of potential ways.

If some writers still seem to be rushing through their books, you can pause them and say, "I notice three things that make this page difficult to read. See if you can find them and fix them. If you're not sure what they are, remember you can reread out loud and listen for places that don't quite sound right."

You will also want to be ready to channel kids toward tools that you have on hand. One of the big ways that human beings evolved over generations is that we began to make better use of tools—and your writers would be wise to make better use of tools as well. Take, for example, the word wall. Some kids actually ignore it altogether, and write even the words that are highlighted on the word wall as if they were inventing those words for the first time. Celebrate kids' tendency to give things a go, but then make sure they know they needn't—and actually, shouldn't—invent when a solution is just a few inches away.

You can also prop kids' enthusiasm up for this work by giving a particular individual an editing pen—perhaps a thin marker pen of some unusual color.

Mid-Workshop Teaching

During the mid-workshop teaching, you might suggest that children take a look at their titles and headings and take some time to revise and edit those as well. One tip you could give is that a heading needs to match the teaching on the page. Perhaps earlier revision work changed the content of the page so much that the chapter needs a new title. You could also remind writers to study the way other nonfiction authors title

Link: Working on being an editor

their books and chapters. Often these titles are fun and catchy. For example, instead of titling a chapter "What Cats Eat," they might title it "Munch! Crunch!"

SHARE

In the share, you and your students can celebrate! You may decide to set writers up in circles of three to four kids and invite them to conduct a "Meet the Author" celebration. This bend encouraged writers to become like the authors in their library, so getting a chance to play that part will bring your rally cry full circle. You might begin by giving everyone some tips for a "Meet the Author" celebration: authors can introduce their books by explaining what inspired them to write about their topic, they can share information from their "about the author" page, they can read their favorite chapter, and they can end with a minute or two for questions. Children can take turns getting up in front of their circle, becoming the celebrated author for a few minutes.

Once writers have celebrated their books with their circle, you might ask them to spend the rest of the share talking about all that they have learned so far as nonfiction writers. Perhaps they will mention how they learned to generate and collect ideas, or how they now know they can pick up any nonfiction book and read it like a writer, gathering tips and ideas to use in their next book. You may want to take a few minutes to collect children's suggestions and add these to the anchor chart. That way, as you launch the next bend, kids can take all that they have learned and apply it to the writing they will do going forward.

Best of luck,
Valerie and Jen

(Samples of students' published books follow.)

—pair up with partner— share— What did we notice?

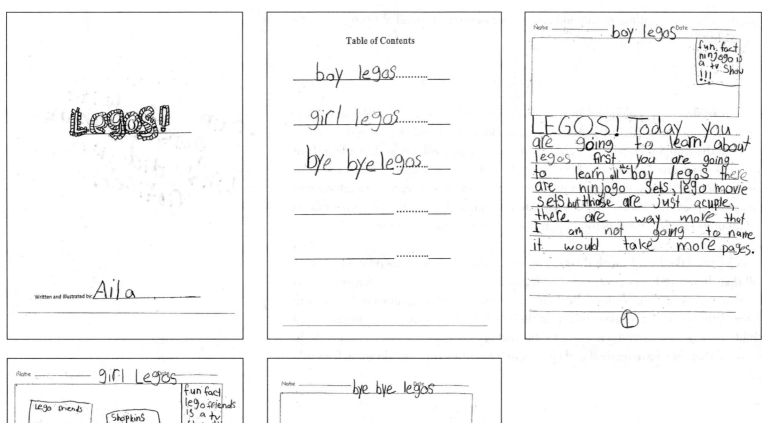

Table of Contents

boy legos

fun fact ninjogo is a tv show !!!

LEGOS! Today you are going to learn about legos first you are going to learn all the boy legos there are ninjogo sets, lego movie sets but those are just acuple, there are way more that I am not going to name it would take more pages.

①

Written and Illustrated by: Aila

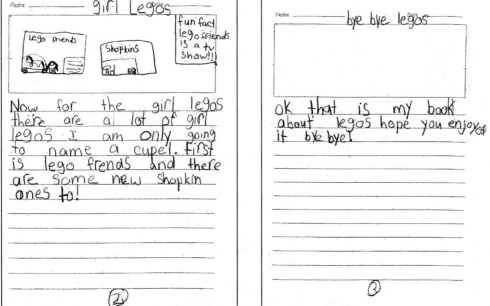

girl legos

fun fact lego friends is a tv show!!!

lego friends   Shopkins

Now for the girl legos there are a lot of girl legos I am only going to name a cupel. first is lego frends and there are some new shopkin ones to!

②

bye bye legos

ok that is my book about legos hope you enjoyed it bye bye!

③

FIG. 5–1   Aila's published book about Legos shows how she used a mentor text to organize her book and add fun facts.

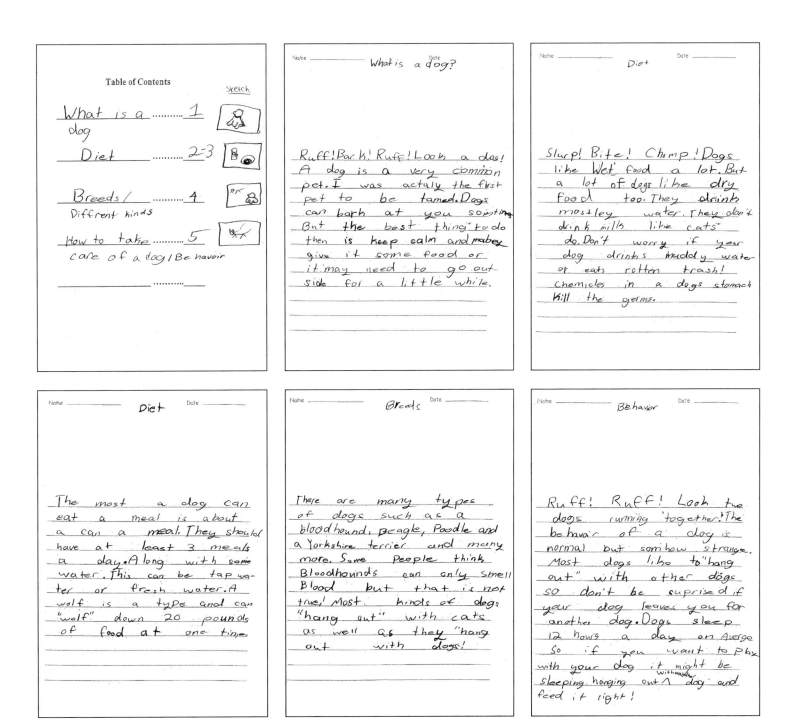

Table of Contents

Sketch

Name _____   What is a dog?   Date _____

Ruff! Bark! Ruff! Look a dog! A dog is a very common pet. I was actuly the first pet to be tamed. Dogs can bark at you soisting. But the best "thing" to do then is keep calm and mabey give it some food or it may need to go out side for a little while.

Name _____   Diet   Date _____

Slurp! Bite! Chomp! Dogs like wet food a lot. But a lot of dogs like dry food too. They drinks mostley water. They don't drink milk like cats" do. Don't worry if your dog drinks muddy water or eats rotten trash! chemicles in a dogs stomach kill the germs.

Name _____   Diet   Date _____

The most a dog can eat a meal is about a can a meal. They should have at least 3 meals a day. Along with some water. This can be tap water or fresh water. A wolf is a type and can "wolf" down 20 pounds of food at one time.

Name _____   Breeds   Date _____

There are many types of dogs such as a bloodhound, Beagle, Poodle and a Yorkshire terrier and many more. Some people think Bloodhounds can only smell Blood but that is not true! Most kinds of dogs "hang out" with cats as well as they "hang out" with dogs!

Name _____   Behavior   Date _____

Ruff! Ruff! Look the dogs running "together! The behavior of a dog is normal but somhow strange. Most dogs like to "hang out" with other dogs so don't be suprised if your dog leaves you for another dog. Dogs sleep 12 hours a day on Averge so if you want to play with your dog it might be sleeping hanging out ∧ dog and feed it right!

FIG. 5–2   Emilia's published book about dogs reflects her ability to "squeeze her brain" adding additional information to each chapter.

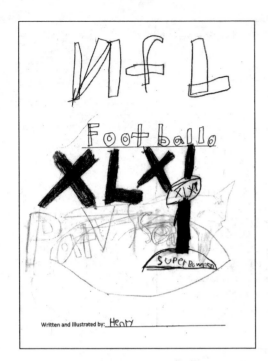

NFL

Footballl

XLXI

Super Bowl XLVI

Written and Illustrated by: Henry

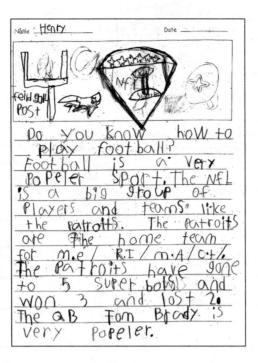

Name: Henry   Date _____

feild goal
post

NFL
Super Bowl

Do you know how to play football? Football is a very popeler sport. The NFL is a big group of players and teams. like the patroits. The patroits are the home team for m.e / R.I / m.A / C.t /. The patroits have gone to 5 super bowls and won 3 and lost 2. The QB Tom Brady is very popeler.

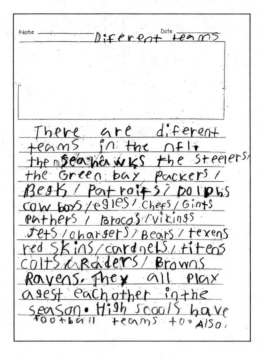

Name _____   Date _____
Diferent teams

There are diferent teams in the nfl. the Seahawks the steelers, the Green bay packers, Beks / Patroits / Dolphs / cow boys / egles / chefs / Gints / pnthers / Brocos / vikings / Jets / chargers / Bears / texens / red skins / cardnels / titens / colts / Raders / Browns / Ravens. They all play agest each other in the season. High scools have football teams too. Also,

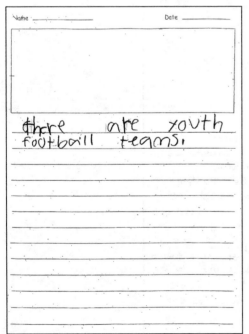

Name _____   Date _____

there are youth footbaill teams.

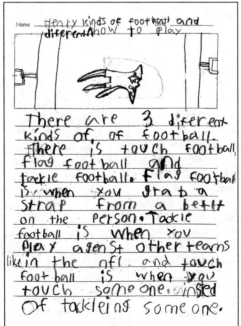

Name   Henry   kinds of football and
diferent how to play

There are 3 diferent kinds of of football. There is touch football, flag football and tackle football. Flag football is when you grab a strap from a beltt on the person. Tackle football is when you play agenst other teams like in the nfl and touch football is when you touch some one insted of tackleing some one.

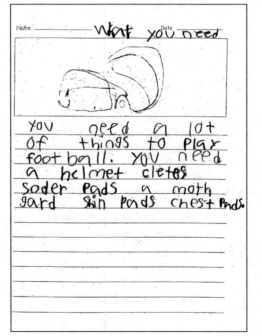

Name _____   Date _____
Wat you need

You need a lot of things to play football. you need a helmet cletes soder pads a moth gard shin pads chest pnds.

FIG. 5-3   Henry's published book about NFL football shows his ability to choose topics of interest and include words that show he's an expert on that topic.

Nonfiction Writers Consider What Information Their Audience Wants to Know

IN THIS SESSION, you'll teach children that when nonfiction writers are writing for an audience, they first think of who their audience will be and then write the information that audience would want to know.

GETTING READY

✔ Writing folders with new writing booklets (see Connection)

✔ Tiny Topics notepads (see Connection)

✔ Your demonstration writing text, starting with only a title, to show students how to write for an audience (see Teaching)

✔ "To Teach an Audience" anchor chart (see Link)

✔ Information Writing Checklist for grades 1 and 2 (see Conferring and Small-Group Work)

✔ Revision flaps and tape (see Mid-Workshop Teaching)

P EER INTO ANY PRE–K OR KINDERGARTEN CLASSROOM during choice time, and you will see kids entertaining audiences of all kinds: a row of bears, a collection of dolls, one another. During recess, a child might hold an audience of peers captive as she bravely propels herself across the monkey bars, landing with a proud bow. That same child will later demonstrate her best reading strategies in a conference as her teacher looks on. Kids adore an audience.

The second bend of this unit plays into kids' understanding of what it means to create for others. If Bend I taught writers to crank out lots of information books, writing them quickly and making sure to use some basic organization skills while writing those booklets, Bend II aims to teach writers to lift the level of that writing, slowing it down a bit and taking more into account as kids write for others. Now, writers will not only choose topics, they will choose an audience too. Children will learn to provide information the audience wants to know, to write in a way that hooks and holds their audience's attention, and to structure their writing so that it's clear enough for their readers to follow and to learn from.

In this session, you invite writers to begin writing for an audience by comparing writing to dancing. As you'll explain, when a person dances for himself or herself, that dancing tends to be carefree, unstructured, and perhaps somewhat messy. When dancing for an audience, however, the dancer's level of preparation and performance changes in big and important ways. In issuing an invitation to write for others, you essentially communicate that kids need to become more thoughtful and intentional as writers.

You will teach a variety of strategies across this session and others to help children keep audience in mind. If you peek ahead to the mid-workshop and share, you will see that these teaching moments invite writers to revise if they have missed opportunities to angle their books toward their audience.

Today, in big ways and small ways, you will apprentice students into the art of writing for others.

Nonfiction Writers Consider What Information Their Audience Wants to Know

CONNECTION

Take a moment to acknowledge the good work that writers completed in Bend I before turning their attention to the work of this bend.

"Writers, can you bring your Tiny Topics notepads and your folders over to the rug? Make sure your folders have a brand-new writing booklet inside! Yesterday was an exciting day. You met the other nonfiction authors in our classroom." I gestured toward the rug. "Nonfiction authors of class 203B, quickly stand up and take a bow." The class followed that direction.

Compare dancing for an audience to writing for an audience, explaining that when writers write for an audience, they rehearse to be clear.

"Can I ask you something? Have you ever danced in your bedroom, all alone when no one was watching?" Kids looked around at each other, a bit puzzled, and started giggling and nodding. "I thought so! What did that dancing look like? Stand up, quickly! Show me!" I stood up and starting dancing in a carefree, crazy way. The kids laughed and followed suit.

After a few seconds, I gathered them back together and we all sat. "Wow! That was some fast and silly dancing! There were arms and legs all over the place. Now writers, have you ever seen professional dancers dancing on a stage? Maybe at a show or on TV? Those dancers look quite different than you do when you dance alone in your room, don't they? Those dancers prepare for an audience. They move their bodies just so."

"Writers, I bet you're wondering why we're talking and thinking so much about dancing. Well, here's the thing: dancing is similar to writing. When you write just for yourself, often your writing is quick and passionate and messy. Just like the dancing you do alone in your room!" I shook my shoulders back and forth playfully to mimic dance moves.

"But, when writers are writing for an *audience*, their writing looks different, just like dancing looks different when it's on a stage or TV—when it is performed for an audience." I sat up pin-straight and lifted my chin as if performing. "'Onstage' writing is clear because it is created for other people—an *audience*."

◆ COACHING

Notice that you begin by creating a drumroll around the work that children have completed in Bend I. At the start of a new bend, it's important to acknowledge the successes children have had leading up to this juncture—and to let them know that those successes position them to now tackle new challenges in the upcoming bend.

Rally students to become the types of nonfiction writers who write for an audience.

I leaned in and said, with emphasis, "During the first part of the unit you were writing for *yourselves*, quickly, only worrying about getting information onto the page, just like dancing around your bedroom.

"That was an important *first* step of this unit. Here's the exciting news. During the rest of the unit, you will be writing nonfiction books for an *audience*. And that means that you'll learn and do all sorts of things to make sure that your writing is like that best onstage dance performance. Once you've written for an audience, your books will be *really* ready to become a part of our classroom library." I pointed back toward our "Class 203B Authors" bin.

"To get ready for your first 'performance,' take out your Tiny Topics notepad and let an idea for another nonfiction book come into your mind." I left a pool of silence. Speaking quietly, I said, "When you have your idea, give me a thumbs up."

I waited until many thumbs went up, signaling that many children had thought of a topic. "Writers, now that you have your topic in mind, you need to put one more thing into your mind. Before you can write, you not only need to have a topic in mind, you also need an audience in mind."

❖ **Name the teaching point.**

"Today I want to teach you that writers write differently when they are writing for an audience. Before they write a chapter, they pause to think, 'What information does my *audience* want to know?'"

TEACHING

Tell your children they're lucky because right there in the classroom, they have what writers need most—an audience.

"So, writers, you ready to write? Think, 'Do I have what I need?'"

I left a pool of silence, hoping children would think about whether they had what they needed to write. "Are you thinking about whether you have a pen, some paper?" Kids nodded, and I did as well. "That's important, right? But writers, the point I want to make today is that just like you need a pen or a computer when you write, you also need to have someone to write *for*. You need an audience.

"And you are super-duper lucky, because right here in this classroom, you have people who can be your audience, if you want to write for second-graders. And if you want to write for grandfathers, could some of you pretend to be grandfathers so you could help each other?" The kids were game.

If you see a lot of kids without ideas for their next nonfiction book, you can prime the pump

TP: Audience

T:

Explain that you're writing a new book for an audience of teachers. Recruit kids to role-play being teachers and then, using them as an audience, demonstrate how your plan the information they would want to learn.

"So listen. I have an idea for a new book. I want to write a book on bakeries." I held up a booklet with the title *Bakeries* written across the top and placed it under the document camera. "I want to write this book for the other teachers in our school, because you know how they crave the yummy treats I bring to school!

"I'm wondering if you could help me write for my audience, the teachers in this school. Let's give it a try. You'll need to pretend to be a group of teachers. Quick, fix yourselves up so you sit and look like teachers." I waited as the kids straightened up, placed on imaginary glasses, grabbed imaginary clipboards. "Listen to my book—while pretending to be teachers—and tell me if it gives you the information you want to learn."

I picked up my book, and scanned the room. "I'm so glad I've got a room full of 'teachers' because I'm just starting a book that is *for* teachers. Will you listen to what I'm thinking of writing and help me get information you want to learn? I know that you're curious about the delicious treats I bring to school. Will you help me think about what you 'teachers' really want to know about great bakeries?"

I winked at the class and they giggled. I turned to a chapter titled "Great Bakeries" and read the title, which was the only thing I'd written.

"Hmm, . . . a chapter on great bakeries." I pointed to the top few lines of the chapter. "So, what might I say here? I know! How about if I tell about one day when I got lost on the way to a bakery, and it was sort of drizzling, and I started to get a bit wet . . . Thumbs up if you teachers would want that information!" I scanned the room, noted a sea of veto signals, and gave myself a thumbs-down sign based on the reaction. "Oops! That's nothing at all about what makes a bakery great, right?

"Hmm, . . . Here's another idea that I'd love to see if you 'teachers,' my audience, would want to learn about. I'm thinking of writing about those awnings that people hang outside their bakeries—you know, the fabric they hang out there that acts like a store umbrella? Would *that* be information you'd want?" Again the kids panned my idea.

After suggesting several kinds of information that the kids reject as information the audience would not want, settle on a plan for information that your audience *would* want to learn.

"You're right. You want to hear all about the treats at bakeries, not about the awnings! My ideas aren't working very well. My plan was to teach all about great bakeries. What makes bakeries great are the delicious baked goods you get there!

"This time I am going to start by thinking about you, my audience, and pretend I am talking to you, telling you information about great bakeries that you'd want to learn." I looked my audience in the eyes, leaned in to them, and this time said, "Some bakeries make a whole lot of different things, but some specialize in just one thing. There are bakeries that just make cupcakes, or just meringue pies, or just bagels."

You will want to begin a new demonstration text today. This book is important as you will model new strategies on it throughout this entire bend. If you decide to choose a topic other than bakeries to write about, make sure it is one that is both engaging to students and that they have some experience with as you will want to recruit their help often as you write this book.

The plan will be for you to propose a few bits of information that your audience is not *likely to want to learn about, so be sure when you produce your proposals, your voice doesn't make these bizarre bits of information seem relevant. Your whole point is to show kids that you are weighing what they will need to teach the reader and putting that information into the book.*

I stopped and checked my audience again, asking with my eyes whether that seemed better, and signals indicated that yes, it was.

Debrief by naming what you demonstrated, that writers can consider their audience to decide what information should be in a chapter.

"Do you see how I first thought about my topic, then about my audience? I let my sense of what my audience—in this case, teachers—would want to learn help me to choose information to write about in my book. That is work that writers do all the time when they go to write information books, or teaching books."

ACTIVE ENGAGEMENT

Channel students to choose an audience. Ask one partner to be the writer and name the information that will go in his chapter, keeping audience in mind; the other will be an audience and provide feedback.

"Writers, now you are going to work as partners to be a practice audience for each other! Before you do this, will you each remember what you are writing about?" I gave the children a few seconds to focus again on their topics. "When you think about what you are writing, be specific. What chapter will you write today? What will be the title of that chapter?" I again gave children time to think. "Now think about who you are writing for. Are you writing for kids in this class? Your family? Teachers? Little kids? Right now, tell your partner who your audience will be." The room filled with a buzz.

"Now that you know what your topic is, and who your audience will be, your job is to think about the specific information that your specific audience will want to learn. Right now, quietly, will each of you think about what *specifically* your audience will want to know about your topic?" I gave children some quiet time to think about that.

"Partner 1, will you pretend it is writing time? Write in the air, knowing that Partner 2 will be your audience. Partner 2, nod your head or give a thumbs up when you think Partner 1's information is something that his or her audience will want to know. Use your hands to gesture for your partner to tell you more good information."

LINK

Suggest that even though children often have a person who can act as an audience, they can use today's strategy even by themselves, making it transferable to any situation.

"Writers, I'm not going to give you time to switch roles, with Partner 2 teaching Partner 1, because I know you are itching to write. And here's the thing. You don't need to actually teach someone—you can just think about what you *would* teach someone. You can plan your writing out so that it works for an audience and *you* can be your own test audience. This is important, because even though a partner makes a helpful practice audience, you might not always have that person nearby. When you're writing for an audience, if there is no one to talk to—no one to be your pretend

Notice that when you debrief this time, you are essentially repeating the teaching point. When you return to the teaching point in a mini-lesson, you emphasize to students that today's learning isn't just about this day or this piece of writing, but is rather an important element that they should add to their repertoire of knowledge to draw upon whenever they write—today, tomorrow, or on any other day.

Notice that we do not take turns, with both Partner 1 and Partner 2 teaching the other his or her content. Instead one partner functions as teacher, the other as audience. By the time you have done that, kids have gotten your point and it is time to move on. Next time, switch the roles that the two partners play.

It's important that children develop the ability to envision an audience without having that group present. This matters not only here, in this one unit, but in other learning environments, and in other scenarios, too. Rarely do writers have the luxury of having a target audience present that they can poll.

audience—you can just *think* of an audience. Maybe it's your Grandma, or the kindergarten class down the hall, or even your dentist! Whoever it is, picture your audience and then, as you write, think, 'What information would my audience want to know?'"

Invite children to begin writing and remind them to carry on with planning strategies from Bend I while undertaking the new, important work of keeping an audience in mind.

"You ready to write? Be sure to write a table of contents and then put the title of the chapter on each page. More than that, be sure you plan how you will write for your readers. Instead of writing like a crazy bedroom dance, you'll be writing for an audience, keeping that group in mind and thinking, 'What would my audience want to know?'" I revealed our new anchor chart.

ANCHOR CHART

To Teach an Audience

- Think, "Who is my audience?" and "What will they want to learn?"

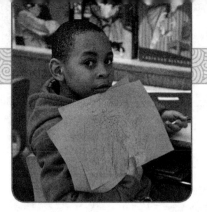

Keep Writers Writing

THIS IS A NEW BEND, so today's conferring and small-group work will in some ways resemble that which you did at the very start of the unit. That is, your first job will be to move quickly among writers, recruiting their energy for the work they've just embarked upon. At this point in the unit you also know a thing or two about each writer. The good thing about today's conferring and small-group work is that you can count on the fact that your writers will be planning. They'll all be engaged in that work; by tomorrow, they'll be in more disparate places as writers. Approach today poised to remind writers to draw on all they learned earlier in the unit as they position themselves for this next bit of writing, and be ready to remind writers to plan and write with audience in mind.

Remind writers to draw on all they know and extend their strategies.

During Bend I, you may have taught some kids that it can help to draw quick sketches of the content they are considering putting into a chapter. If so, you will want to remind those students to continue using this strategy in their new books. Now when they sketch, though, you will encourage them to consider which subtopics will interest their audience.

FIG. 6–1   Lily uses sketches to plan her table of contents for her book about dogs that is intended for new dog owners.

MID-WORKSHOP TEACHING
Writers Reread to Add More Information for Their Audience

"Writers, I want to give you a quick tip about writing for an audience. When you write for readers, after you finish a chapter, it is important to reread that chapter and to think, 'What *else* might my audience want to learn?'

"Right now, squeeze your eyes shut and imagine your audience. When you can see that person or group, clear as day, start rereading your chapter, slowly and carefully—sentence by sentence. The rereading you'll do is a special kind of rereading, because when you reread, you'll pretend to be people who don't know about your topic, or younger kids, or grown-ups, or the dentist— or whoever your audience is! When you get to a place where you realize, 'Wait! My audience would want to know more right here!' mark that spot and keep reading. Then in a few minutes, you can come back to the spots you have marked and add more to them."

After kids worked for a few minutes, I said, "Writers, even if you haven't finished rereading your draft pretending to be your audience, it's time to shift back to your writing. I've put some flaps and tape onto your tables in case some of you have revision work to do right now. Get to work, writers!"

You may invite these writers to apply this strategy to their table of contents by suggesting that they sketch subtopics for their whole book. After writers have made some initial quick sketches for a chapter, you can offer them another tip: "Writers, you know that quick sketches can help you plan a *chapter*, but did you also realize that sketches can help you plan your *whole* book? You can grab a blank piece of paper and sketch some of the important subtopics you think your audience will need and want to know about your topic. Each sketch can represent something new you will teach about your topic. Then, as you write, you can always look back at your table of contents and look for the next sketch as a reminder of what you want to teach."

You have emphasized rereading several times throughout the unit already. Today you might encourage students to use rereading as a way to develop subtopics for their books. You may notice some students stuck trying to develop a table of contents or pausing after one chapter trying to decide what an audience would like to know next. To support these writers you might say, "Writers, it's important to think about your audience, but it's equally important to actually write! Sometimes writers don't have a plan for their book at the start—that's okay! When this happens, writers just start writing; they don't wait and wait and wait for a plan to come. After a bit of writing, though, they look back and reread what they wrote in their first chapter. Then they think, 'What will my audience need or want to know in the next chapter—right after reading this one?' Writers keep going like this from one chapter to the next, building a plan, and the book, as they go!"

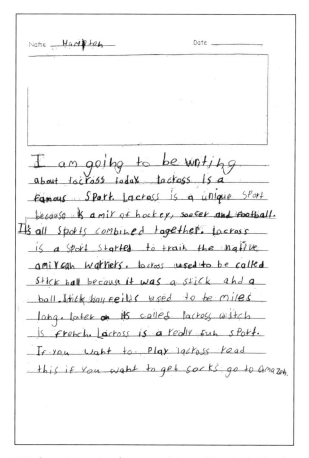
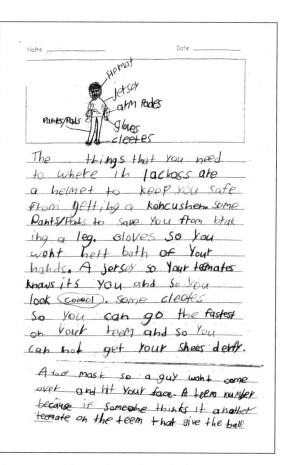

FIG. 6–2   Hampton began writing without a table of contents. He started by teaching about the history of lacrosse and then switched subtopics by turning the page and teaching about the materials needed for lacrosse.

Encourage writers to use checklists from the start.

The last bend ended with writers using checklists to drive their revision work, but checklists can also support writers as they begin to draft new books. Today as you move from table to table, remind writers to set their checklists out alongside their writing. Explain how checklists can help them write for an audience. You may point to parts of the checklist and say, "Writers, you used to just think about the important points and parts of the topic *you* wanted to teach. Now when you plan, you need to think about the important points or the parts of your topic that will be helpful or interesting for your *audience*. When you think of something new to teach your reader—something he or she would want to learn about—you can add onto your writing." I pointed to the elaboration section of the Information Writing Checklist. "Your writing can have different kinds of information such as facts, definitions, details, steps, and tips. As you write with your checklist alongside you, remember that you are working toward these goals with your audience in mind!"

If you have been teaching from the Units of Study in Opinion, Information, and Narrative Writing series, you will have access to *Writing Pathways* and to the full sequence of checklists. You'll definitely want to bring out the third-grade checklist for a few of your stronger writers, since every writer will profit from having crystal clear horizons to work toward. Take a few moments with these writers to clarify how the expectations for third grade differ from those for second grade. Encourage these students to reach for these increased expectations from the start.

Name: _____ Date: _____

Information Writing Checklist

	Grade 1	NOT YET	STARTING TO	YES!	Grade 2	NOT YET	STARTING TO	YES!
	Structure				**Structure**			
Overall	I taught my readers about a topic.	☐	☐	☐	I taught readers some important points about a subject.	☐	☐	☐
Lead	I named my topic in the beginning and got my readers' attention.	☐	☐	☐	I wrote a beginning in which I named a subject and tried to interest readers.	☐	☐	☐
Transitions	I told different parts about my topic on different pages.	☐	☐	☐	I used words such as *and* and *also* to show I had more to say.	☐	☐	☐
Ending	I wrote an ending.	☐	☐	☐	I wrote some sentences or a section at the end to wrap up my piece.	☐	☐	☐
Organization	I told about my topic part by part.	☐	☐	☐	My writing had different parts. Each part told different information about the topic.	☐	☐	☐
	Development				**Development**			
Elaboration	I put facts in my writing to teach about my topic.	☐	☐	☐	I used different kinds of information in my writing such as facts, definitions, details, steps, and tips	☐	☐	☐
Craft	I used labels and words to give facts.	☐	☐	☐	I tried to include the words that showed I'm an expert on the topic.	☐	☐	☐
	Language Conventions				**Language Conventions**			
Spelling	I used all I knew about words and chunks (*at, op, it,* etc.) to help me spell.	☐	☐	☐	I used what I knew about spelling patterns (*tion, er, ly,* etc.) to spell a word.	☐	☐	☐
	I spelled the word wall words right and used the word wall to help me spell other words.	☐	☐	☐	I spelled all of the word wall words correctly and used the word wall to help me figure out how to spell other words.	☐	☐	☐

Information Writing Checklist (continued)

	Grade 1	NOT YET	STARTING TO	YES!	Grade 2	NOT YET	STARTING TO	YES!
Punctuation	I ended sentences with punctuation.	☐	☐	☐	I used quotation marks to show what characters said.	☐	☐	☐
	I used a capital letter for names.	☐	☐	☐	When I used words such as *can't* and *don't*, I put in the apostrophe.	☐	☐	☐
	I used commas in dates and lists.	☐	☐	☐				

Revising Table of Contents Pages for an Audience

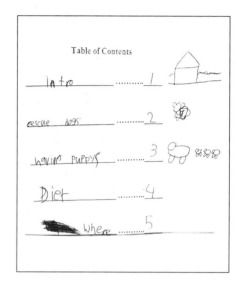

Suggest that writers keep in mind what an audience would want, starting with the table of contents.

I called the class to the rug, and as writers began to find their spots I said, "When you get here, will you make sure your book is open to the table of contents page?" Once kids were settled with that page open, I said, "When nonfiction authors write for an audience, they consider what information their audience wants every step of the way—starting with the table of contents. I see many of you have started to write the table of contents for your book." The kids looked down onto their laps, nodding yes.

Set partners up, once again, with roles: one as the audience for the other. Invite children who are in the audience role to provide feedback on the presenting partner's table of contents.

"Before you plan any further, let's take advantage of our practice audience!" I pointed toward the class, indicating that they should still use each other. "Right now, meet back with your partner, only this time, switch roles. Partner 2, *you'll* be sharing. Partner 1, you'll pretend to be Partner 2's audience. Listen to Partner 2's chapter titles and then give feedback on your partner's table of contents by thinking, 'What do you, the audience, want to learn?' Are there chapters your partner left out, ones with information you'd want to learn? Are there chapters your partner should change—maybe they don't really belong in this book after all?"

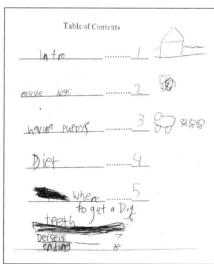

As children did this work, I circulated, coaching Partner 1s as they gave feedback to Partner 2s. "Is there anything else you'd want to learn?" I prompted. "What other chapters might you (the audience) want?" and "Will that chapter have information the audience would *really* want to read?"

After a few minutes I called for the class's attention. "Writers, eyes back up. As you move forward in your nonfiction books, remember the importance of your table of contents, your plan. You can always add to it or change it based on what your audience would want to know. Take a few moments now to revise your plan so it's ready to go for tomorrow!"

FIG. 6–3   Maxwell revised his table of contents after meeting with his partner, his "practice audience," and considering what his audience would want to know.

Helping Readers Picture Information

IN THIS SESSION, you'll teach children that once nonfiction writers have considered who their audience will be and what information that audience would want to know, they think, "How can I help my readers picture the information?"

GETTING READY

✔ Student writing that has been revised to include more description (see Teaching)

✔ Student writing folders and writing in progress (see Active Engagement)

✔ "To Teach an Audience" anchor chart (see Link and Mid-Workshop Teaching)

✔ A collection of high-interest nonfiction books that are popular in your room (see Conferring and Small-Group Work)

✔ "How to Play: Can You Picture It?" one-day chart (see Share)

✔ Your demonstration writing from Session 6 to show students how to write with detail (see Share)

NOW THAT YOUR KIDS are deeply immersed in writing nonfiction for a specific audience, keeping in mind what the information is that the audience will want to know, you may want to talk with them about how to hold that audience's interest. All of your writers have at one time or another read a nonfiction book. You can remind them that nonfiction readers can often tell whether a book will be boring or interesting almost from the first few pages. This session suggests that you demonstrate what it looks like when a reader loses interest in a book, contrasting that with an enactment of what it looks like to be engrossed in a book. If kids join you in playacting the engaged reader, you'll see them sit up straighter, turning their imaginary pages with more fervor. This is the way kids want others to read their books.

In today's minilesson, you'll more specifically emphasize that writers hold their readers' interest by helping those readers picture whatever it is that they need to see. Is this a book about picking apples? If it is, the reader needs to see the bright, shiny color of the apples hanging from the trees. They need to smell the sweetness in the air and hear the crunch as a bite is taken.

Later, in the mid-workshop teaching, you'll remind writers that they already know another strategy for helping their readers picture information—using comparisons. The share will bring all of this together, by inviting partners to work together to add more details to their descriptions. This second bend of this unit will draw on your partnerships almost daily as writers work to craft books for an audience. If you have not yet used partners during writing workshop, you may want to spend a few minutes considering the children who will work best together and partnering them. At the Reading and Writing Project we usually recommend pairing students who feel comfortable talking and sharing their work with one another, playing off of your social capital. We also recommend that these partners stay together for at least the duration of the unit, if not longer.

Helping Readers Picture Information

CONNECTION

Engage students in acting out what it's like to read a boring book. Explain that writers work to write books that keep audiences interested.

"Has anyone in this room ever read a *b-o-r-i-n-g* book?" When hands sprang up across the meeting area, I feigned surprise. "Really? So many of you! Right now, will you pretend to be reading a book that is ever so boring and show me what *you* look like when you read a *b-o-r-i-n-g* book." The kids commenced a great drama.
After half a minute, I intervened. "Readers, now will you show me what it is like when you read a super-interesting book? Act out that kind of reading." The kids sat up straight, and began that drama.

"So, writers, whenever you write anything, the goal is to make sure that your audience reads your book like this," I reenacted their vignette of reading a super-interesting book, "and *not* like this." I reenacted the image of a bored reader that some had shown me, holding a book, letting it flop on my lap as I pretended to fall asleep. The class giggled.

❧ Name the teaching point.

"Today I want to teach you that writers don't only think, 'What information will my audience need to know?' They *also* make sure to hold their readers' interest by thinking, 'How can I help my readers picture the information?' Writers do this is by using description."

TEACHING

Tell a story that illustrates how using descriptions can help a reader picture information.

"Let me tell you a quick story. My sister has been teaching me about cooking, and yesterday she taught me how to make guacamole. The most important step is choosing the right avocado! She didn't teach me in an unclear way by just saying, 'You choose a good one.' She taught me in a way that helped me to picture the information—the avocado I should choose. She said, 'To choose an avocado that is ready to eat, first look at the outside. It should be very dark green and bumpy. If it is bright green, smooth and shiny, it isn't ripe yet!' Then she said, 'When you pick up the avocado, it shouldn't be hard when you squeeze it. It should feel firm, but soft.'

Exaggerate. Have some fun. Be over-the-top. Your goal is to make your minilesson memorable and engaging—and to a large extent, that depends on your delivery.

You will, of course, want to craft your own story here as an example of how people use descriptions to teach others. Notice, though, how we use many adjectives throughout the vignette. This is deliberate. You want your story to really drive home the point that descriptions are both helpful and interesting.

"Writers, when my sister described what an avocado should look like and even feel like, I could picture what she was saying in my mind. Nonfiction writers do exactly what my sister did all of the time. They use descriptions—how things look, how they feel—to help their readers picture their subject."

Show an example of how a student author uses descriptions to help the reader picture information.

I held up Zachary's writing from the previous day. "Writers, yesterday when Zachary was teaching his audience—his little brother—about Spider-Man, he decided that his brother would want to learn about Spider-Man's webs, so he wrote this":

> Spider-Man can shoot webs out of his wrists.

"After Zachary wrote that, he thought, 'Wait a minute!' How will my brother know what the webs look like or feel like?' So he decided to give this part of his book another go. This is what Zachary wrote next."

> Spider-Man can shoot long and sticky white spider webs out of his wrists.

"Writers, do you see the difference that second version makes? Do you see how Zachary helped readers picture his information? Zachary described what Spider-Man's webs look like and even how they feel. That description of the webs—*long and sticky*—really helps you picture them! Can't you see in your mind what that looks like?"

Children nodded enthusiastically.

"I know that Zachary's brother will be able to picture those webs in his mind, too. There's no way he'll be falling asleep while reading this book!"

ACTIVE ENGAGEMENT

Set writers up to practice this strategy in their own books.

"Are you ready to try this out on your own? Right now, put your book on your lap and open to the first chapter you'll work on today. It might be one you started yesterday or a brand-new chapter. Either way, you'll want to bring your audience into your mind so that as you begin writing, you can include descriptions in a way that will help that audience picture the information. Plan the information that will go in your chapter and then think, 'Which pieces of information do I need to help my readers picture? How can I describe it?' You might choose to tell your audience how things look or how they feel. Give it a try right now!"

Coach students to rehearse descriptions orally before writing in their own books.

I moved around the room, whispering in prompts. "Help people picture what it looks like." "What does that feel like? Help your readers know." "Say your description aloud even before you write it."

You will want to make this second part of the teaching section your own as well by choosing to highlight the work of a specific student in your class. Today your teaching did not lean on demonstrating the teaching point but rather highlighting it by using two different examples.

As you set kids up to try this work in their own writing, give some coaching tips up front as children are searching through their own writing. That way, children have had both thinking time and some advice before they dive into trying the work out in their books.

When I crouched down near Eric, he said, "I'm closing my eyes so I can see a truck. They have huge wheels!" I prompted, "Zoom in closer on the wheels, what else do you see? You can think about color and shape, too." Before Eric could tell me how he'd add onto his idea, I leaned over to coach another child, so that Eric would talk to his partner instead of to me.

I moved close to Gayle as she felt her braid, leaned over to her partner and whispered, "It has big bumps that are smooth." I leaned in to coach, "Touching the thing you're trying to describe seems to be helping! How else can you help readers picture your braid?"

LINK

Remind children that as they continue to write for an audience, they should now be doing so in ways that help their audience picture the information.

"As you write for your own audience today, make sure that you aren't just keeping in mind what that person—or group—needs to know, but also that you include vivid descriptions to keep the readers' interest and to help them picture the information! You don't want them falling asleep while they read your books, do you?" The class immediately shook their heads no.

"I didn't think so! Let's add this to our chart."

ANCHOR CHART

To Teach an Audience

- Think, "Who is my audience?" and "What will they want to learn?"
- **Help readers picture the information.**
  - **Add description.**

"I know that using descriptions will help readers picture the information, but I'm also thinking there are some other ways that authors help readers picture the subject. Will you keep your eyes open for other ways to help readers picture the subject, and to keep your readers wide awake? If you find other ways, let the class know.

"As you go off to write today, remember that even though you are writing 'onstage' nonfiction books, it is still your job to teach your audience as much as you know about your topic. Don't let writing for an audience stop you from filling your books to the brim with information, but this time, think about how you can make those chapters better than any you have written before. Off you go."

Notice how I move around the rug quickly, giving tips to lift the level of students' descriptions, but not staying to hear how their revised ideas sound. That is okay. The point here is to coach many kids in a short amount of time. I am always keeping my eye on the clock!

Help readers picture information:

Add description

Add comparisons

Issuing an invitation for writers to discover other strategies is tucked into the link so that students are reminded to take responsibility for their own learning. In the first bend you encouraged students to look to mentor authors as a way to learn more about nonfiction writing. You will want to keep this invitation alive across the unit through little reminders like this one.

Varying Small-Group Methods and Structures

AT THE START OF THIS BEND, most of your kids were at the same place in their writing—planning and starting new books. By today, they'll each be doing different work. Some of them will have whipped through a quick, underdeveloped book and will be eager to write "about the author" sections and call it a day. Those youngsters will need encouragement to either revise those books or to start new ones. Other youngsters will be producing a few longer chapters a day, and will be working on their third and fourth chapters in the books they began at the start of this bend. They will need support adding new strategies to their repertoire as they write so that each subsequent chapter reflects more of the work of the bend.

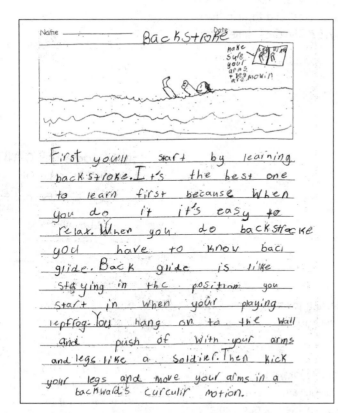

FIG. 7–1   Ebby took a cue from the minilesson and used descriptions to help her reader picture information as she wrote her chapter about the backstroke.

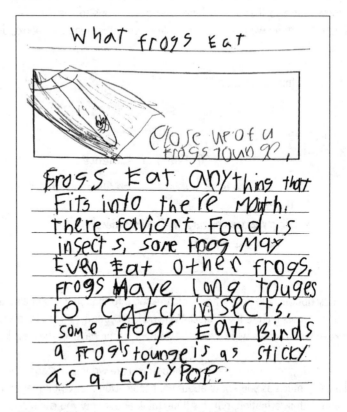

FIG. 7–2   Marc uses comparisons to help his reader picture how sticky a frog's tongue can be after hearing the mid-workshop teaching.

Standing in the midst of the workshops, I asked for the class's attention. "Writers, pretend I was writing a book about you. I could talk about the way you are all working away by saying, 'The room 203B is filled with hardworking kids,' but that doesn't really help people who don't know you picture just how hard you work, just how special this room feels.

"So I've been thinking about how I can give people a picture of you all, working so hard. How about this: 'Writing workshop in room 203B is like the inside of a busy beehive.' I bet comparing you all—working so hard—to bees working in a hive will help people who don't know you picture you all writing away. Comparing one thing to another is one more way to help readers really picture the information.

"Right now, reread down your page, and see if you can find a place to compare the information in your chapter to something else. It should be in a place where you're trying to help someone—your mom, best friend, or whoever your audience is—picture the information! Give it a try while I add this strategy to our chart."

ANCHOR CHART

To Teach an Audience

- Think, "Who is my audience?" and "What will they want to learn?"
- Help them picture the information.
  - Add description.
  - **Add comparisons.**

Help readers picture information:

Add description

Add comparisons

busy as

Children will not only be at different stages of their writing, they'll also need lots of different instruction. That is, although your minilesson championed the importance of using description to help readers picture the information, you'll have some youngsters who write a word and then take a break, thereby never writing with fluency or voice. You may need to coach those writers to think of a whole sentence, then write that whole sentence without pausing. Other writers will be combining a host of different topics into a single chapter, and will need to be reminded that writers reread, checking to make sure they've sorted their information so that it is bucketed.

Today, as you prepare for your conferring and small-group work, you might rehearse not only the topics you might teach, but also the methods you might use. It is helpful to have a bunch of these at your fingertips. For example, if you find a bunch of kids would profit from similar instruction, you might gather a small group and suggest the kids watch as you confer with one child. After conferring, you can extend the teaching

by saying to the observing children, "Might some of you be willing to try what so-and-so is going to try?"

Then again, you could simply catch a youngster in the act of doing something that you wish others would try as well, and you could rally others to see what the one child has done. "Can I show you what so-and-so just did that some of you might try?" Then you will need to story-tell the steps of what the one child has done. If, in fact, you helped the child to do that work, take yourself out of the story. So instead of saying, "I told her to reread her writing," say, "Then she decided to reread her writing." In this way you can take the work that one child has done, celebrate the work making it her own, and extend that work to other writers.

Another method for leading small groups is an inquiry. Sometimes it is helpful for writers to see the kind of writing they are trying to do. Perhaps some youngsters have not yet realized that their new books need to look and sound different from their

(continues)

earlier attempts. Gather them together to study an example of the kind of writing an audience wants to read—take your cues from kids during reading time and choose the books they are pouring over as readers. Invite kids to study these texts together—to point out what makes them so engaging and interesting, and then encourage them to look at their own books for places where they might try this work as well.

A third way of leading small groups may involve gathering writers to participate in a peer response group. You could gather several partnerships and set children up to alternate between reading their writing and giving each other feedback. If you decide to do so, you may channel children to give feedback on specific things. For example, you might channel kids to check to see whether all the information in a particular chapter goes into that chapter, or might some of it address a different subtopic. Remind writers that when they give feedback, it is often helpful to point to the specific lines in the text that they are discussing and to provide a suggestion for one possible way the writer might fix things.

Adding More Detail to Descriptions

Introduce students to a game to help them write with detail. Have them try a round with you and then play with their partner.

"Writers, you know when you write a really great Small Moment story, readers can make a movie in their mind, picturing what you are saying? Well, when you write a really great information book, readers can picture what you are teaching them. But for readers to picture your subject, you need to write with a lot of detail. When Zachary wrote, 'Spider-Man can shoot webs out of his wrists,' I had a hard time picturing what he was teaching me about Spider-Man, but when he wrote, 'Spider-Man can shoot long and sticky white spider webs out of his wrists,' I could picture it, couldn't you?

"So I was thinking you could test your writing to see if it has enough details—it can almost be like a game. The writer finds a place where his or her writing *should* give the reader a picture, and the writer reads that part of his or her writing to a partner, and the listening partner tries to picture what the writer is saying. If the partner can't picture it, he or she can ask the writer for more details." I pointed to where I'd written the process out on chart paper.

"Let's try it with my book. I'll be Partner 1. Let me look through my book about bakeries to find a place where I hope readers can picture what I am saying." I glanced at my writing, and pointed to show that I had found such a part, then I clutched my book to my chest to ensure no one could see.

"Now I'll read you my descriptions, and you tell me if my descriptions are clear enough that you can *really* picture what I'm writing about." I paused and looked at my writing.

> The cupcakes are delicious. They have a lot of frosting. Yum!

"Can you *really* picture what I'm writing about?"

Several kids shook their heads no. "What *kind* of frosting do they have?" Raymond wanted to know.

"Oh, I forgot to add that! Some have chocolate frosting and others have vanilla. Let me add that to my writing." I started to jot the new information but then Lily interrupted.

Lily asked, "What does the frosting *look* like?"

Setting writers up to play a "game" is one way of engaging kids in the work of writing. Show them that drafting and revising can be playful and fun!

"The frosting is on the top of each cupcake, and it has a swirl that makes it look almost like a soft ice-cream cone. Oh, and some cupcakes even have rainbow sprinkles on top!" I looked at my page for a micro-second and then said, "Hey! I'll add those details later to make my writing even more specific. Listen to how it will go and then tell me, after I write the new way, will you picture it?"

> The cupcakes are delicious. Each one has a swirl of chocolate or vanilla frosting on top, looking almost like a soft ice-cream cone. Some cupcakes have rainbow-colored sprinkles.

The kids nodded yes. "Are you ready to play the game yourselves?"

"Yes!" the kids chorused.

"Here's the trick. Partner 1, if you need to say *more* than you wrote, you'll need to add those details to your writing. Okay, get started!"

As children played the game, I channeled the clue givers to remember to revise their books, adding in any new descriptions, comparisons, or specific clarifying details that they needed to give their partners.

Nonfiction Writers Aim to Hook an Audience's Interest ... Right from the Start!

T HINK ABOUT THE LAST PIECE of nonfiction writing you read. Perhaps it was a news article, a blog post, your Twitter feed, or a favorite magazine. Ask yourself what it was about that piece of writing that made you want to read it. Chances are it wasn't just the factual information that held your attention. Rather, it may have been the writer's voice or tone—or maybe it was the style he or she assumed. Consider this: with the exception of perhaps furniture assembly instructions, most nonfiction writing aims to entice. Nonfiction writers know they need to hook their readers and keep them reading.

Today's session helps writers do just that, as well as continue the work the class began yesterday. In the last session, you taught writers to help the audience picture the information. In this session, you'll build on that work by teaching kids to hook their audience right from the start. Today's minilesson channels kids to investigate how writers build interest through chapter leads. In the mid-workshop teaching, you invite writers to discover ways to make the ends of their chapters interesting, too, so that readers want to turn the page to learn more.

One big goal, not just for today but throughout this bend and the next, is that your students produce books and chapters that look and sound markedly different from the ones they produced in the first bend. In Bend I, students wrote quickly to teach as much as they could about a topic. Their books contained lots of information but only a bit of elaboration. Now, you'll expect to see your writers working with greater deliberation to craft chapters that include the specific information an audience would want to know and that incorporate new elaboration techniques. The strategies you are teaching are ones that *all* nonfiction writers use, not just second-grade nonfiction writers. Therefore, your students' writing should start to more closely resemble the nonfiction books they are reading. The work they are assuming may slow some writers down a bit, so be sure to keep an eye on volume—children should be producing multiple books with lots of chapters across the bend. Most writers should be wrapping up their first book by the end of today and ready for a new one tomorrow!

IN THIS SESSION, you'll teach children that nonfiction writers grab their audience's interest from the start of a chapter with an interesting lead.

GETTING READY

✔ A nonfiction text—we use *Extreme Sports* by Sean Finnegan, but you may choose another nonfiction book with a powerful hook at the beginning of each chapter. Ordering information for *Extreme Sports* is available on the online resources (see Teaching)

✔ "To Teach an Audience" anchor chart (see Teaching)

✔ A chapter from your demonstration text, beginning with a weak lead that students can help rewrite (see Active Engagement)

✔ Revision strips and tape (see Active Engagement)

Nonfiction Writers Aim to Hook an Audience's Interest ... Right from the Start!

CONNECTION

Celebrate your children's efforts to make nonfiction books interesting.

"Yesterday you learned that writers don't just write for an audience, thinking 'What will my audience want to know?' They work hard to help readers picture the information. Are there writers here who have described what something looks like? What something sounds like? How something moves?" Thumbs popped up around the rug.

❧ **Name the teaching point.**

"Today I want to give you another tip for keeping your readers interested. If you want your reader's attention, you need to grab it right away. Nonfiction writers make sure to grab their audience's interest, to hook their audience, right from the start."

TEACHING

Recruit the kids to join you in examining how an author writes leads to various chapters, making sure the leads are ones that hook readers.

"Writers, let's take a peek inside of *Extreme Sports* and think about what Sean Finnegan does to hook his readers." I made a hand gesture to illustrate the idea of hooking a reader. "At the beginning of each chapter, he writes a lead that he hopes hooks his reader." I opened the book to page 2, and revealed the lead to a chapter called "What Are Extreme Sports?"

"Read with me and as you do, think about *how* Sean's lead to this chapter hooks his audience. How does the lead get his audience wanting to read on? Ready?" In unison, we read,

> *Have you ever heard of bungee jumping, skydiving, or snowboarding?*
>
> *These are all kinds of extreme sports.*

"So, what do you think? How did Sean Finnegan write his lead so that it would pique his audience's interest?"

◆ COACHING

Notice that this connection references the work the class did in the previous session. You'll want to do this often—to explicitly link a new day's teaching to the teaching that came before it. This accomplishes two things: first, it helps children understand how to build on what they've done earlier, and second, it reinforces the idea that teaching and learning are cumulative.

Sometimes it helps to invent a gesture to accompany your point—especially when it is a point that you really want kids to remember and cite often. Perhaps, for example, you can turn your hand into a giant hook, drawing the kids (the readers) toward you as you make the point.

You'll only be able to support shared reading here if you are able to enlarge the print, perhaps with a Smart Board or a document camera. It is also okay for you to just read this aloud.

"He asked a question!" offered Joey.

"You are right! In this lead, Sean hooked his reader by asking a question. That is how he hooked his audience right from the start. It's almost like Sean Finnegan is inviting his readers to join a conversation. Let's see if he uses any other strategies for getting the audience interested." I turned to page 12. "This one is called 'Extreme Air Sports.'"

Skydivers travel high up into the sky in an airplane and then "dive" out of the plane.

"That lead is much different! Hmm, . . . What has Sean Finnegan tried here?" I let my voice trail off, inviting students to offer a response.

"He told us what skydiving was like and made it sound cool!" said Raymond.

I clarified Raymond's language to name a transferable strategy. "Oh, so he *introduced* skydiving to his audience so we could picture what it is?" The class nodded.

"And he uses words that pop out—like *travel high up* and *dive*—to make the topic sound interesting?" Again, kids indicated yes.

"So already you have two great ways to start your chapters so that you can hook your audience's interest right from the start." I revealed the chart from yesterday and added the new strategy.

> **ANCHOR CHART**
>
> ### To Teach an Audience
>
> - Think, "Who is my audience?" and "What will they want to learn?"
> - Help readers picture the information.
>   - Add description.
>   - Add comparisons.
> - **Hook readers with an interesting lead.**
>   - **Ask a question.**
>   - **Introduce the chapter's topic with pop-out words.**

"You could ask a question, or you could introduce the topic of your chapter."

Students will often need support in naming writing strategies in transferable ways—they don't have the same language and experience we have as adults! To support their approximations, listen carefully to what they notice in a text. Then think about how you can name out the strategy in a way that your whole class can understand.

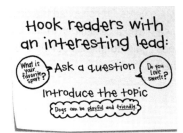

ACTIVE ENGAGEMENT

Engage students in writing a lead using one of the two strategies you've just taught.

"You'll remember that the other day I wrote a chapter about where to get the best bakery treats. Let me look at how I started it." I picked up my draft, and read in a flat voice.

> I get my treats at different bakeries. I get cupcakes at Magnolia Bakery.

"Hmm, . . . Is this hooking my reader, a group of teachers?" "I'm not sure it does that too well. Writers, will you talk to each other and see if some of you could come up with a better lead for my chapter?"

As partners turned to each other, I listened in and recorded one of the livelier lead ideas I heard on a revision strip. "Writers, Sasha suggested I begin with, 'Have you ever wondered where to get the very best baked sweets?' What do you think? Would that hook you in and make you want to keep on reading?"

As kids nodded, I added, "Yes, especially if you are an audience who has a sweet tooth." I quickly taped my new lead down in place.

Notice how you now make the strategies learned in the teaching transferable by asking kids to help you use them in your writing. Often when students uncover a new craft move in a mentor text, they have trouble transferring it into their own writing. By providing immediate practice, kids are one step closer to using what they have just learned in their own work.

LINK

Channel students to plan out multiple leads for a chapter in their own nonfiction books.

"Writers, before you head off, quickly open to a chapter in your book. After you have your audience in mind, plan a few different leads on your fingers, one lead for one finger, and think, 'Which lead would my audience find the *most* interesting?'"

Remind writers that they need to hook their readers' interest at the beginning of each chapter.

After only a few moments, I reconvened the class and said, "Writers, most of you have three, even four chapters already written. That means you'll remember to hook your reader at the beginning of every single one of your chapters." I reached out, once again, to mimic hooking the reader by the collar and drawing him in, gesturing for the class to join me. "Okay, writers. Off you go!"

Writing to Capture the Interest of Your Audience

TODAY'S MINILESSON launched writers into one of the trickiest jobs any writer will ever have—the job of keeping an audience interested. It is no small task to captivate and hold an audience's interest. Many professional writers struggle to do this. And young children tend to be egocentric, so it is especially challenging for them to imagine the perspective of a reader who is different from themselves. The good news is that your children will have plenty of opportunities and be given loads of strategies to help them tackle this work.

Encourage writers to add their own thinking as a way to create interest for their audience.

The simplest way to think about whether kids are writing for readers is to check whether the kids have tried to make their writing interesting. If your students experienced the first-grade information writing unit *Nonfiction Chapter Books* last year they were taught to try to add something interesting to every page, and you might remind

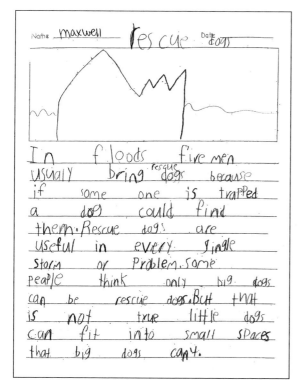

FIG. 8–1   Maxwell adds in his thinking among facts to keep his audience interested in his book about dogs.

SESSION 8: NONFICTION WRITERS AIM TO HOOK AN AUDIENCE'S INTEREST . . . RIGHT FROM THE START!

67

kids of that prior instruction. It's a good goal! Another way to help kids aim to interest their reader is to help them realize that usually a mere catalog of facts won't be as interesting as a mix of facts and ideas.

You might have some writers who seem to think that the main job of a nonfiction writer is to teach facts. In that case, you might remind them that in reading workshop, they've learned that when readers talk about books, they do more than just recap the text. In kindergarten, your readers learned to lift the level of their partner conversations about books by shifting from retelling to "adding a pinch of themselves." They did this by including what they thought or how they felt about the book they were reading. You'll explain to writers that this isn't something readers, alone, do—writers can aim to "add a pinch of themselves" as well! Nonfiction writers can make information interesting for an audience by simply adding in some of their own thinking.

If you have a chart with thinking prompts from reading, have it close by as a reference. If you don't yet have a tool of this sort, decide on just a few phrases to share with writers so as to not overwhelm them. You might jot a few phrases such as: "This is important because . . . ," "This shows that . . . ," or "The surprising thing about this is . . ." on a chart for writers to reference. To give writers a bit of practice, invite them to help you add some thinking into your teacher text on bakeries. Perhaps you will turn back to the chapter you wrote about great bakeries, reread a bit, and then ask kids to help you add in some of their thinking. Then you can invite writers to try this strategy across a few pages or chapters of their own books. Have revision strips on hand at the tables or in the writing center so that writers can easily revise their writing to include a bit of their thinking.

Remind writers that they can add tips and warnings for their readers.

Writers can also engage their readers by thinking about added tips and warnings that they may need to insert so as to inform their readers. If your children have grown up within the Units of Study books, they'll have experienced this work during the kindergarten *How-To Books: Writing to Teach Others* unit and learned to add tips or warnings, as needed, into those books. When detailing how to make toast, the kindergarten writer may have added 'Don't touch the red part inside the toaster or you will burn your fingers!' Now, writers can again add tips and warnings for readers: "Remember to . . ." or "You should . . ."

Channel writers to draw on all they know as they write and revise their work.

Of course, although the minilesson focuses on writing with readers in mind, your youngsters will need to draw on all they know about writing in general and information

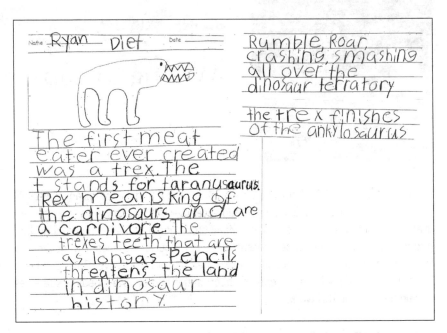

FIG. 8–2   Ryan revises his lead to hook the reader into his chapter about a dinosaur's diet.

writing in specific as they work, and it will be important for your conferring and small groups to help them keep prior instruction and previously set goals in mind. It is likely, for example, that a few of your second-graders are still producing only a page or two a day. You might investigate this a bit more by reading the few chapters they have produced. Perhaps these writers are overly concerned with only teaching what an audience will want to know or writing to make each sentence interesting. If this is the case, then you will want to teach them that they can draft a chapter quickly, as best they can for an audience, and then go back to make revisions. Volume and repeated practice are priorities for second-grade writers, so you will want to help these students set goals and make plans for writing double and even triple their current amount. Then, too, if some of your youngsters aren't remembering to spell the high-frequency words they almost know with accuracy, coach into that. Always be sure that your conferring and small-group work is responsive. At the Teachers College Reading and Writing Project, we often tell principals that one way to assess a teacher's teaching during work time is to check and see if the teacher is teaching responsively and not simply repeating the day's minilesson.

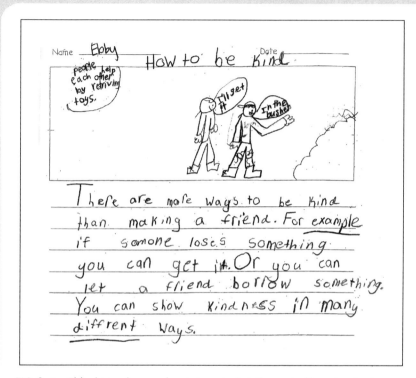

FIG. 8–3   Ebby keeps her readers interested at the end of her chapter by leaving them with a big idea.

Standing in the midst of the writing workshop, I asked for kids' attention. Once all eyes were on me, I said, "Writers, I love that you guys aren't just doing what I talk to you about in the minilessons, but that you are also inventing your *own* ideas for ways to make your books interesting to your audience. Some of you have been telling me that you are working to make not just the start of your chapters, but also the *end* of your chapters hook readers and make them want to continue reading. Holy moly! I'm going to have to go get another job because you are teaching yourselves.

"If any of you want to borrow my copy of *Extreme Sports* and study what Sean Finnegan did to interest his readers at the ends of chapters, that'd be cool. You could teach the rest of the class what you find. I'll leave the book up here. And meanwhile, keep inventing your own ideas for ways to make every page of your book as interesting to readers as it can possibly be."

Recruiting Help from an Audience
Reading Chapters to Partners

Invite one writer to share his writing with the class and voice over about techniques used to interest readers. Rally partnerships to read their work and give feedback.

I invited the class back to the rug—writing in hand—where I had a surprise waiting for them. "Writers, you have been working to write with an audience in mind for a few days now, but you haven't really done this work with help from an audience.

"For a few days now, you've been reading and rereading, rehearsing your chapters for only yourself. Dancers do this before a big performance, too. They practice over and over all by themselves. But, here's the thing, dancers also practice in front of other dancers. They do that so their performance will be perfect for the big night. Writers, I was thinking you all could do this, too!"

I gestured toward the space on the floor, where I had used painter's tape to mark off a big square. "Here is *our* very own stage. John, could you hop up onstage and read your book to this audience?" I gestured toward the class. "And class, as the audience, let's listen especially for whether John's lead hooks us in and whether he writes in ways that keep us interested."

I handed John an imaginary microphone, and gestured for him to read the first chapter of his book. As he did so, I voiced over parts where John had clearly hooked his audience and written interesting information down the page, in ways that the rest of the class could transfer to their own writing.

After John was done and had taken a bow, I said, "Writers, am I right that you'd all love to practice onstage, just like John did?" As kids eagerly waved their hands in the air, begging to be called next, I said, "There are so many of you that one stage isn't enough! Could you take your partner and find a place in the room where you two can make your very own imaginary stage? Partner 1, get up on that imaginary stage and read one of your chapters for Partner 2! Partner 2, keep doing that same kind of listening, noticing how Partner 1 hooks you from the start and keeps you hooked. Give your partner tips for how he or she could make the book even stronger. Get to it, writers!" Kids scurried off to different parts of the room and began to tap into the benefits of an audience.

FIG.
wait
book
...ers rehearsal of his or her book

Make this playful rehearsal even more purposeful by whispering voice-overs to the rest of your students. Name the work that one student did as he rehearses, thus turning it into another model for the rest of your class.

Session 9

Writers Do More Than One Thing at Once

Making Writing Interesting and Keeping One's Audience in Mind

I N A SOCCER MATCH, players alternate between dribbling, passing, and shooting the ball. A player dribbles toward an opponent's goal, passes the ball to a teammate, and then repositions for a shot at the goal. In some ways, nonfiction writing is a bit like playing soccer. A writer also has to use different skills, alternating between them at a moment's notice. For instance, a nonfiction writer has to consider the content an audience wants to know, organize the content with a clear plan, and then teach it in a way that will keep the reader turning pages. A writer works down the page like a soccer player works across a field. And just as a peewee soccer player is approximating the seamless style of play you might see at World Cup level of play, so too are young writers approximating toward what published, adult nonfiction authors do.

In today's minilesson, you will teach writers to orchestrate more than one strategy as they write. Some writers may be writing with their audience uppermost in their mind, trying to get bits of information the audience wants to know onto the page. Other writers may prioritize keeping their audience interested through catchy leads and comparisons. Still other writers are focused on sounding out words and getting things spelled. Today you will inform writers that they need to try to do all these things, all at once. Writers can remind themselves of the various tasks that need to be juggled by making cue cards or other reminders.

In the mid-workshop teaching, you will highlight how writers can orchestrate multiple strategies not only as they write, but also as they reread and *revise*. If they reread and find they have written chapters that were light on specific information or descriptions, they can decide to revise to add the missing element.

Today's share will be particularly important! Just as a live audience gives feedback through applause, gasps, and laughter, partners will read each other's books and leave feedback through Post-it reactions. These may be comments like "Wow!" "Gross!" or "Hmm, . . . ?" Be sure to leave time for this important work at the end of your workshop today, as it will provide a springboard for your next minilesson.

IN THIS SESSION, you'll teach children that writers give themselves reminders to keep their audience in mind while they simultaneously work to generate interesting writing.

GETTING READY

✔ Your demonstration writing with a new chapter titled but otherwise blank (see Teaching and Active Engagement)

✔ Student writing folders, Post-its, and a pen (see Link and Share)

✔ By the beginning of this session, students should have written one book during Bend II and be ready to begin a second one. For tips on supporting your students in increasing their writing volume, see the Conferring and Small-Group Work section.

✔ "To Teach an Audience" anchor chart (see Teaching and Active Engagement, Link, and Share)

✔ Post-its for you and the class to create reminders (see Teaching and Active Engagement) and for children to leave each other feedback (see Share)

✔ Large Post-it notes, chart paper, and markers (see Share)

Writers Do More Than One Thing at Once

Making Writing Interesting and Keeping One's Audience in Mind

CONNECTION

Challenge children to pat their heads while rubbing their stomachs. When they struggle, point out that it is similarly hard for writers to think about audience while making their writing interesting.

"Writers, hurry to the meeting area because I have something cool to tell you," I said, adding that they should bring their folders, some Post-its, and a pen. Once the kids had settled, I said, "Can you pat your head? Do that now."

Giggling a bit at the odd command, the children did as they'd been told. "Now rub your stomach in a circle," I said. As the children stopped patting their heads to rub their stomachs, I called out reminders: "Do both at once." "Don't *rub* your head—pat it!"

In no time, the kids all agreed it was very hard to do those two things at once. "Just like it is hard for any of us to *both* pat our head and rub our stomachs—doing two things at once—it is hard for writers to *both* make their writing interesting *and* keep their audience in mind. And you know what? Yesterday when I asked you, 'What are you working on as writers?' *not one kid* said, 'I'm thinking about how to make sure my audience wants to know the information I am sharing!' You were so busy writing interesting leads or teaching important facts, that it almost seemed like you forgot your readers altogether!"

✤ **Name the teaching point.**

"Today I want to teach you that writers make sure to keep their audience at the front of their minds the whole time they are writing. To do this *and* teach interesting facts, they give themselves reminders that help them do two jobs at once."

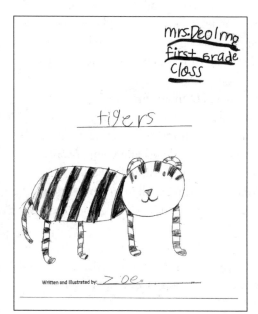

FIG. 9–1   Zoe places a Post-it with her audience written on it on the cover of her book. This will remind her of who will read her book about tigers.

The challenge to pat their heads and rub their stomachs simultaneously is a fun, memorable way for children to grasp the concept you are teaching: that sometimes writers must do two things at once.

TEACHING AND ACTIVE ENGAGEMENT

Suggest that creating a reminder can help children keep their audience in mind as they work to make their writing interesting. Invite them to do this, then model it on the demonstration text.

"So, writers, I was thinking that if you had a reminder to help you think about your audience, even as you work to teach interesting facts, maybe you could do two jobs at once. You guys are so creative. I bet you could come up with a reminder. Will you talk together and see what you can invent?"

After a moment, I shared one idea I'd heard. "Writers, I want to share Brit's reminder idea. She plans to write the name of her audience—*kindergartners*—on a Post-it with a picture of children underneath. What a great idea for an audience reminder!" I took out my own Post-it, quickly wrote *teachers* across the top, drew a picture of a few teachers underneath, then placed the Post-it on my bakery book.

Invite partnerships to help you write a chapter in your demonstration text, using a reminder Post-it to keep the audience in mind while making the writing interesting.

"There, now I have my own reminder. Now let's put it to the test. Could you help me write another chapter for my bakery book? Let's see if this reminder will help us do two jobs at once—teach interesting facts *and* keep my audience in mind." I turned to a new chapter in my book titled "After-School Treats" as the kids agreed to help.

"While we're writing, let's use our 'To Teach an Audience' chart to remember some ways to keep our audience in mind *and* make our writing interesting. Partner 1, why don't you take the job of keeping the audience in mind? Partner 2, could you be in charge of making the information interesting?

"To get started, Partner 1, make sure my audience—teachers—is in mind." I pointed toward the chart. "What facts will teachers need to know about after-school treats? Partner 2, how can you make the lead interesting? You'll have to work together, partners, to do both jobs. Give it a try!"

As each duo started discussing what my lead might sound like, I leaned in close to Brit and her partner. "I think teachers need to know what to get from the bakery to eat as a snack after school." I prompted her partner, Max. "How could you turn that information into an interesting lead?" I looked back toward the chart. Max said, "What if it said, 'Have you ever wondered which bakery treats are the best after-school snack?' Brit nodded in agreement as I called the class back together.

Share out examples of partners' writing that is both interesting and mindful of the intended audience. Invite children to add on and double-check that the information satisfies both goals.

"Writers, Brit and Max were thinking I should write 'Have you ever wondered which bakery treats are the best after-school snack?' That's definitely information that *teachers*—who are hungry for a snack after a busy school day!—would want to know, right?" I pointed toward my Post-it reminder. "And Max thought starting with a question would make the information interesting!" The class concurred and I quickly wrote the idea down on the page.

There are several methods of teaching that you will use in your minilessons across a unit. You may notice that a predominant method is demonstration, but there are other effective methods as well, such as explain and example, guided inquiry, and guided practice. Today we chose to use guided practice in the form of shared writing. Using shared writing in today's minilesson allows your writers to enter into the rehearsal part of the writing process alongside you. Students think, talk, and construct parts while you coach in and eventually compose, or write their ideas.

Asking partners to work together at first, here in the teaching and active engagement, is a subtle but important move. Later on in the link they will try this same work, doing two things at once, in their own writing. They are apt to be more successful later on because of the scaffolding partnerships provided here.

After-School Treats

Have you ever wondered which bakery treats are the best after-school snack?

"Hmm, . . . okay, what should I write next? What are the facts that the audience would want to know, and how could I write this in a way that is interesting? Turn and talk—see if you can do both jobs at once!"

As kids began talking, I leaned in to a few partnerships, collecting their ideas and ensuring that students were remembering both to keep the audience—teachers—in mind and to make their information interesting. I pointed toward the reminder Post-it at the top of my chapter and also channeled kids to look toward the chart, reminding them of strategies they had learned. After a minute, I called the class back together.

"Writers, as I tell you what I heard, what my next few sentences should be, let's do a double-check. Put one thumb up if the information is what the audience—teachers—would want to know and put a second thumb up if it's interesting. I heard some of you share that the next few sentences should go like this." I read aloud from my chapter.

After-School Treats

Have you ever wondered which bakery treats are the best after-school snack? Cookies are great choices because they are small and sweet, but they won't make you too full for dinner.

As I spoke, kids slowly raised one thumb, then two into the air. "Well, it seem like we've done both jobs again! Teachers would want to know that cookies are a great choice for an after-school snack, and your description of cookies as 'small and sweet' makes the information interesting. Thank you for your help!"

Debrief. Point out that a reminder helped children do two things at once.

"Writers, did you see how using a reminder can help writers do two things, two jobs, at once?" I pointed back to the Post-it at the top of the chapter. "You helped me both keep my audience in mind, writing what they would want to know, *and* made the information interesting."

LINK

Set children up to work independently, first making themselves a Post-it reminder, and then writing with the aim of doing two things at once, with the reminder and the anchor chart as a guide.

"Writers, why don't you quickly try this now? First, take a few moments to make your own reminders. Then see if you can write a little bit of one of your own chapters, doing two jobs at once. This time, though, instead of working with your partner, work together with your Post-it reminder and the anchor chart, 'To Teach an Audience.' Give it a try!"

After half a minute I voiced over, "Make sure you're finished making your reminders and start writing your chapter, this time doing two jobs at once! You might stick your reminder right on the top of your chapter to keep you on track."

When you combine the teaching and active engagement, as is often the case for guided practice, it helps to provide students with repeated practice. Notice that during this second turn-and-talk, we release the support to students by providing fewer tips up front. You may decide to use more nonverbal prompts, such as pointing to the chart, so that children learn to take on more of the work without your support.

You'll want to listen in to students and then report back what you heard instead of calling on individual students to share their ideas. This will allow you to move quickly through your minilesson and for the point to remain clear.

Giving kids a few moments to get started on their work right there in the meeting area allows them to experience immediate practice of what they just learned, and it also functions as an opportunity for you to collect a bit of data. Be careful, though, not to get caught up here. Give kids just a few moments and then send them off to continue their work for today.

Debrief. Remind children of the various things they might do as nonfiction writers, and that always, they will keep their audience in mind.

After a few moments, I called students back together. "Writers, as you continue to write nonfiction books, your jobs may change. Sometimes you may try to make your writing interesting. Other times you may be trying to make the information clear. The one job that will never change is writing for an audience, keeping your audience in mind." I pointed back toward the anchor chart, reminding students to use it as a reference.

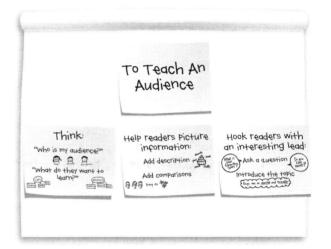

ANCHOR CHART

To Teach an Audience

- Think, "Who is my audience?" and "What will they want to learn?"
- Help readers picture the information.
  - Add description.
  - Add comparisons.
- Hook readers with an interesting lead.
  - Ask a question.
  - Introduce the chapter's topic with pop-out words.

Making Sure Writers Are on Track

TODAY'S MINILESSON acknowledged that it's no small feat to do two things at once when you write. It will be important to check in on how students have been taking on the goal of writing with greater intention—with purpose and craft.

MID-WORKSHOP TEACHING
Writers Check that Their Writing Is Perfect for Readers

"Writers, you've learned that it helps to read your writing for an audience. You've also learned that it helps to make sure you are hooking that audience in by making interesting leads to all your chapters, and to make sure you are writing in descriptive ways so that people can picture what you are saying. But here's the thing. You don't always get a chance to read your writing to a trial audience. And so it is really important to be able to pause in the midst of writing and to think, 'Okay. Now I am going to take on the identity of someone who has never seen this text, someone who knows nothing about this topic.'

"It is amazing but you can pick up your writing, pretending you have never seen this draft before, and you can actually read it as if it is totally brand new to you. And the important thing is that when you do that, all of a sudden you see places where the writer (that's you, but you are pretending it is someone else altogether) hopped about from one thing to another. You can tell where the writer writes without details. You can feel places where the writing is just plain confusing and you find yourself going, 'Huh?'

"So right now—or soon, if you are in the middle of something—take a moment to reread your writing and think about the work you need to do so this writing is perfect for readers."

Meanwhile, be sure that writing with intention hasn't slowed children down to the point of producing just one book. Maintaining writing volume is as important as ever.

The first thing you can look for is whether your students' writing in this bend seems adequately different than the writing they produced during Bend I, when they wrote books that were more like first drafts with some basic revision. In the first bend, they wrote quickly, trying to capture as much information down the page as they could. Writers may have revised by adding a page to a chapter or a revision strip at the end, but that was the extent of their revision. In this second bend, though, your students' books should look and sound like they have been written with more intention. Intentional writing may take the form of chapters with more carefully selected information, or chapters that incorporate several strategies to create interest: hooking the reader with a question and making the information come alive through descriptions, comparisons, and tips.

To take on the more sophisticated work of this bend, some writers may have slowed down and therefore only produced one book. These writers may need help getting started on a second one. Other writers may have shifted from producing writing that looks and sounds more like Bend I writing to creating chapters that are crafted with more thought toward an audience. A closer look at their work may reveal that although they are incorporating the work of this bend into new books, they are doing so one strategy at a time. These writers could benefit from some support using a repertoire of strategies as they write.

Maintain students' writing volume by encouraging them to start new books.

Today is the fourth day of the bend and most writers will have already started a second book. If you find that a few students are still working on their first book of this bend, you will want to take some time today to help them get started on a second book. It's

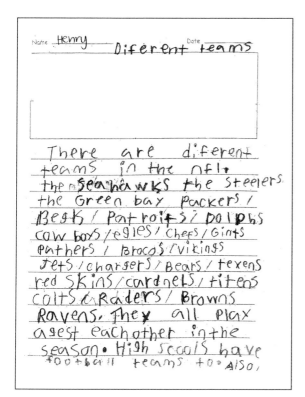

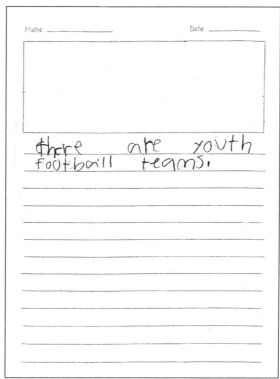

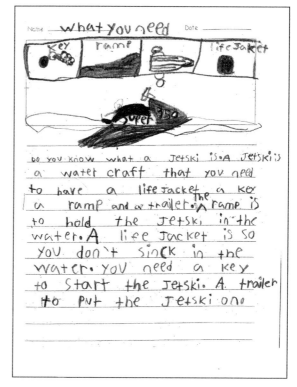

FIG. 9–2 The first two pages of a chapter from one of Henry's books (written during Bend I) contain a few facts and a long list of examples. The third page (from a chapter from a book from *this* bend) shows how Henry has grown as a writer. His chapters now contain a variety of ways he is teaching information.

important that writers have the chance to practice the work of the bend in more than one text. Repeated practice helps writers internalize new work.

You might gather the students who need to begin a second book together in a small group. Although it is typical to start a group by saying, "I called you over because . . ." and then to dive right into work, you might instead begin with a twist. You might begin by inviting everyone to quickly name out their topics in a topic share, singing out their topics into the group, one by one. This will allow you to get a sense of topic choices, help you make recommendations for children's next books, as well as allow other writers to hear topics from their peers—a way to sort of prime the pump for next books.

Once kids have given their topics a quick shout-out, you might say, "Writers, congratulations on writing a nonfiction book crafted with an audience in mind! I know your books are filled with facts your audience will want to know and *also* written in ways that will keep them turning pages. But, writers, you don't want to limit yourselves to writing just *one* book—no way! You have *so much* to teach! You want to write more books. When nonfiction writers are getting ready to start their next book, they have lots of different ways to get ideas. Sometimes, they use their first topic as inspiration; they think, 'What else do I know and want to teach about that is like this topic?' Maybe they wrote a book about dogs and now they're ready to write a book about cats. *Another* way nonfiction authors get ideas is to listen to what other writers are writing about and to think, 'Do I have a topic like any of those topics that I want to

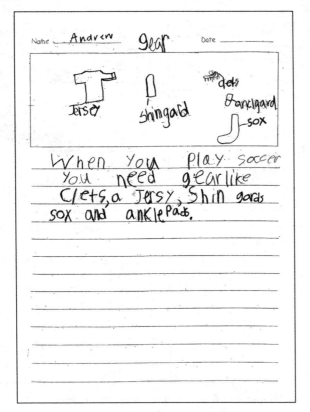

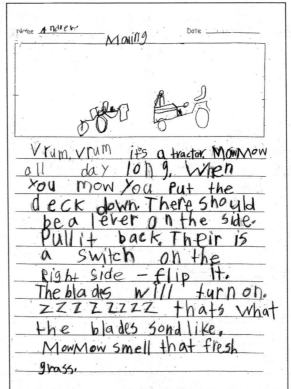

FIG. 9–3   Laying a chapter from one of Andrew's first books on soccer alongside a chapter from this bend on tractors reveals the ways in which he has grown as a writer. He now writes in ways that capture an audience's interest and helps readers picture information.

teach?' Other times, writers have topics on deck and just need to grab a new booklet and go!

"So right now, could you think about your next book? When you have an idea, grab a booklet from this pile right here and start planning!" As kids consider their next books, you might go between coaching for topic choice, giving reminders about choosing an audience, and offering tips for making a new plan.

Support writers to use a repertoire of strategies in more purposeful ways.

You will also want to keep your eyes peeled for kids who only work on whatever you mentioned in that day's teaching point. These kids may rarely mention anything you

taught on previous days when you ask them what they are working on. You will want to notice if kids are adding new strategies into their repertoire each day, or if they are just picking up the work from one day's minilesson but then dropping it the next. It may be there are some students who need support using anchor charts with more intention. Remind writers that they have a repertoire of strategies to draw from, not just an assignment of the day. Students now have two anchor charts they can draw from to remind them of all they know how to do, as well as the option of studying other nonfiction texts for support.

Imagine you pull alongside a child who is following a series of the past few days' teaching points, but who doesn't seem to be transferring what he knows from other times and other days. You might remind this writer, who seems to think each day's work stands on its own, that the real goal is to use everything he has learned to make his writing the best it can be. "Writing can be a bit like juggling," you might tell the child, pantomiming throwing up balls and catching them. "When you juggle you have one ball in the air at first, but then you quickly add another and another. Each ball comes back around and down to your hand to be thrown back up again. When you write, you use one strategy, put it down for a moment, then pick up another and another, knowing that in your next chapter you will come back to all of these again."

You could support this writer to juggle strategies by inviting him to reread a few of his chapters, checking to see if, in fact, the work he is learning in each minilesson is coming back around from one chapter to the next. If he finds some chapters to be lacking, he can mark those chapters with a star or Post-it and plan to revise them later, perhaps with the most recent copy of the anchor chart in hand.

Partners Leave Each Other Feedback

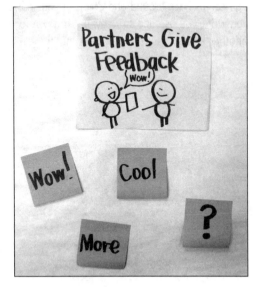

FIG. 9–4   Class-made chart of possible feedback phrases

Set up partnerships to read each other's writing through the lens of their intended audience and leave each other feedback.

"Writers, please join me in the meeting area. Bring your writing folder and a stack of Post-its. All of your books now have several chapters that you've written for an audience. Many of you have several books even. You've read chapters to your partner, but you haven't gotten any feedback from your practice audience! You haven't gotten to hear what is going well and what you should change or fix.

"So right now, trade books with your partner and read your partner's writing. Be his or her audience! As you read, you can use Post-its to leave feedback for your partner. You might write 'Wow!' on shocking parts that taught you something new." I quickly jotted "Wow!" on a Post-it and stuck it up on the easel as a model for students. "Or 'More' on a part where you think your partner's audience would want to know more."

"What about 'Ew!' if the part is gross?" added Lily.

"Definitely!" I added both examples to the easel. "You might also find places where your partner should help you picture the information. Think of the strategies we've learned to guide your feedback," I said, pointing toward the "To Teach an Audience" chart.

"Right here on the rug, swap writing with your partner, use his or her audience reminder to get into character, and then start reading and leaving feedback!"

As the class started writing feedback to each other, I continued to add to the Post-its on the easel examples of feedback writers were leaving for each other. I added "Cool," "?," and "Huh?" for kids to have as mentors.

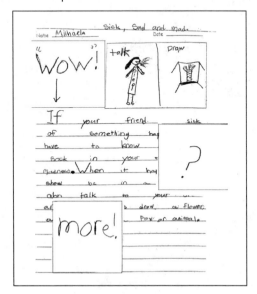

FIG. 9–5   Michaela's partner gives her feedback on her chapter about sleepover problems.

Session 10

Clearing Up Confusion
Answering Readers' Questions

I N MANY WAYS, today's session builds on work your writers did in first grade. In the first-grade writing unit of study, *Nonfiction Chapter Books*, writers learned that to elaborate they might reread their writing, notice places where their readers may have questions, and then add in information to help their readers learn more. Today you will invite your readers to reread, to notice places where questions arise, and then to revise to clear up any confusion. Rereading and asking questions is a powerful combination that will help writers clarify their writing, not just today but for days and even years to come.

During the share in the previous session, partners read each other's books and left feedback. While some of the feedback may have been complimentary—"Wow!" or "Cool!"—some feedback may have been in the form of a question—"What?" or "Huh?" This work specifically set writers up for today's minilesson where you will invite them to reread their own writing and mark places where they have questions to answer. Later, in the mid-workshop teaching, you'll build on this by reminding writers that they may also need to reread their writing looking for places where their spelling or punctuation gets in the way for readers. As students work, you may want to offer up revision tools, such as revision strips or extra booklet pages, scissors, and tape, so that writers can insert clarifying information into the exact spot it's needed.

The share today will bring forward more of the work from the first-grade unit as you teach writers that they can use first-grade strategies in new ways. In *Nonfiction Chapter Books*, writers learned to elaborate by writing in twin sentences, using teaching pictures with labels and arrows, using descriptions and comparisons, and giving examples. Now you will challenge students to use these strategies in more sophisticated ways. Instead of just labeling parts in a diagram, a writer might construct a phrase or sentence next to each arrow and part of the picture. If your writers have not experienced this first-grade unit, then you may choose to add in a day of teaching and practice using some of these strategies together on your teacher text and then invite writers to try them in their own books as well.

IN THIS SESSION, you'll teach children that nonfiction writers make sure their writing isn't confusing for readers. To do this, writers reread, notice when they have questions, and clarify that information.

GETTING READY

✔ Your demonstration text, marked up with a trail of Post-it feedback (see Connection)

✔ "How Can I Teach My Readers?" chart from Grade 1 Unit 2, *Nonfiction Chapter Books* wrapped in layers of tissues. Reveal part of the chart in the connection and the rest in the share (see Connection and Share).

✔ A chapter from your demonstration text, deliberately written in ways that confuse readers, prompting them to ask questions (see Teaching and Active Engagement)

✔ Revision strips and tape (see Active Engagement)

✔ "To Teach an Audience" anchor chart (see Link and Mid-Workshop Teaching)

Clearing Up Confusion
Answering Readers' Questions

CONNECTION

Share examples of feedback a teacher partner left on your demonstration book, calling extra attention to where your partner was confused.

As children gathered with their folders on the rug, I placed my bakery book under the document camera. "Writers, after seeing all of the feedback your partner left you, I thought I should ask a partner to leave *me* some feedback as well! I asked a teacher to read my book, since after all, my audience *is* teachers." I opened my booklet, and made a show of delighting in the Post-it feedback left throughout.

I highlighted one piece of feedback. "Look here, on my first chapter, my partner wrote, 'Wow!' where I wrote about bakeries that sell only cupcakes. I must have surprised my audience with that fact.

"And here, near where I wrote about different cupcake flavors," I pointed to a Post-it marked "More!" and the whole class read it in unison. "I guess my audience wants to know more about flavors. How helpful it is to have readers who give feedback!"

Turning to the next page of my book, I called students' attention to a Post-it that had a big question mark written on it. I paused, taking on a more serious tone, "Writers, this is feedback that an audience only leaves if they're left with questions, and we *definitely* don't want to leave our audience wondering."

❖ **Name the teaching point.**

"Today I want to teach you that when nonfiction writers write for an audience, they make sure to clear up any confusion so that readers are not left with questions. Nonfiction writers do that by rereading as if they were the audience and finding places where they have questions themselves."

TEACHING

Remind kids of instruction they received last year, assuming their teacher taught the Units of Study. Share a teaching point from first grade and suggest that this continues to be important this year.

It's fun for kids to see you, their teacher, receive feedback on your writing. It's important that they also hear you think through the feedback you received, reflecting on what each comment means for your next steps as a writer.

"I was in Ms. Bellino's first-grade classroom yesterday and I found something *amazing*. I stopped in my tracks, stared at it, and then I asked Ms. Bellino if I could borrow it and bring it to you. You ready to see what it is?" The class signaled that they were.

I brought out a packet that, to the kids, was totally mysterious. (The kids will soon find that it is a Post-it, swathed in layers and layers of tissues.) I unwrapped one layer, another, another, building suspense, until a Post-it lay in my hands. "Look at this!" I said, holding it up in awe for all to see. I revolved slowly in front of the class so that all the kids could read the Post-it:

Think About Questions—Who? What? When? Where? Why? How?

"I was *so* thrilled to see this! You know what this told me? You *already know* that as writers, it is important to ask and answer questions. That means you also know that when there are places in a book that are confusing, you can fix the confusion by asking and answering questions.

"Now that you are in second grade, you'll do this work in a more grown-up way." I straightened, proudly, to emphasize *grown-up*. "You won't just write each chapter, hoping you answer all of these questions on every page." I pointed toward the question words listed on the chart. "Oh, no! Now that you are more grown-up writers, you'll reread to find confusing places where you left questions unanswered. Then you'll think, 'What is the question that my audience needs me to answer?'"

Ask children to act as the Question Crew for your book. Share a part, written to be confusing, and then invite partners to name what exactly was confusing.

I pointed toward my bakery book. "Could you all help me by pretending to be my audience of teachers, this time acting as the Question Crew?" They agreed.

"Great! You know that there are some unanswered questions in this chapter, but now it'll be your job to listen for the exact parts that leave you with questions. As I read, if any parts leave you with questions, you might signal to me by giving a little shrug." I modeled the gesture. "Listen closely, Question Crew!" I started reading, making sure to dramatize the parts of the chapter that were vague or confusing.

Bakery Treats for Special Occasions

Have you ever wanted to get a special treat for a special day? Bakeries can make you special treats for some days. They can make you all sorts of things!

After the first few lines, kids around the rug began to dramatically shrug their shoulders, so I paused. "It seems like lots of you *already* have unanswered questions."

"'Some days'? What days?" yelled Jack. Lots of peers nodded in agreement.

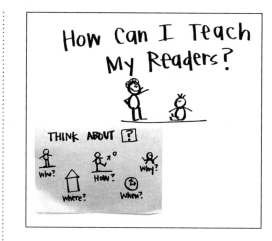

This minilesson references a chart from the first-grade unit Nonfiction Chapter Books. *If your children experienced this unit, point out that today's lesson stands on the foundation of that work. Using Post-its to capture strategies that kids learned earlier is a visual way to remind them that they've done this work before. In the minilesson, you'll only highlight one strategy from the chart, and in the share, you'll reveal the entire chart. If your kids haven't experienced this unit, you'll need to adapt the minilesson to be less of a reminder and more instructional.*

"Oh, so you're thinking that I didn't answer the question, 'What are the special days that bakeries can make you special treats for?'" Again, the class nodded.

"Let's see if I can revise that. I'll add, 'Bakeries will make you special treats not just for your birthdays, but also for Mother's Day, St. Patrick's Day, and Valentine's Day. A bakery will even make special treats for a Writers' Celebration Day!'"

Debrief, emphasizing that writers can spot places where their information is confusing, and then ask and answer questions to clarify for their readers.

"It is important to do the work you just helped me to do as my Question Crew. First you helped me notice a confusing place—a place where there was an unanswered question. You then asked me a question so that I could revise my writing to answer it."

ACTIVE ENGAGEMENT

Ask partners to read more of your book, look for unanswered questions, and then write answers to those questions on revision strips.

"Writers, will you, with your partner, continue to read the chapter from my bakery book? If you get to a confusing place where a question has been left unanswered, pause there and see if you can answer it. Then would you help me by writing *the answer* to that question on a revision strip that I could add into my book? Get to it, Question Crew!"

Bakery Treats for Special Occasions

Have you ever wanted to get a special treat for a special day? Bakeries can make you special treats for some days. Bakeries will make you special treats not just for your birthdays but for Mother's Day, St. Patrick's Day, and Valentine's Day. A bakery will even make special treats for a Writers' Celebration Day! They can make you all sorts of things!

You can order any flavor, but the best part is they decorate in really awesome ways. You can just get a name. But you can also paint a picture onto your cake with frosting. Bakers can make your cake into the shape of a flower, a caterpillar, a tennis racket, a robot—anything! If you want a special treat you need to order it ahead of time so that they can prepare it exactly how you'd like it.

As kids talked, I crouched near partners and listened in. Liam and Matthew pointed up toward the chapter. "I have a question there where it says, 'They can make you all sorts of things.' It doesn't say what sorts of things they make!" Liam said.

Matthew responded, "Yeah! She could add cakes, cookies, and cupcakes, and stuff like that!" He started scribbling onto a revision strip as I moved to the next partnership.

Revision is a multistep process. The teaching works to break down these steps and engage kids in the process alongside you.

Actively revising here will help prepare students later for when they are asked to transfer this work to their own writing.

Show students how you can use revision strips to revise your writing.

After a few minutes I called the class back together. "Writers, you are an expert Question Crew! You found so many parts of my chapter that were confusing, that left you with unanswered questions." I held up a few of the revision strips containing "answers" to questions for the class to see. "Matthew and Liam had the question, 'What special treats can the bakery make?' They wrote, 'Bakeries will make you cakes, cupcakes, and cookies.'" I taped the strip down to my chapter.

LINK

Send students off with a new partner to read their nonfiction books with the intention of clarifying confusing parts.

"Writers, today you'll have your very own Question Crew. Just for today, can you find someone near you on the rug, someone who is *not* your partner, without leaving anyone out? Meet in a group of three if you need to." I sent off half of the class, gesturing the other half to stay and get started working on the rug.

"You'll start today by rereading one book with a new partner and finding places that are confusing or vague. Those who are listening, ask the writer questions so he or she knows just what to add in."

After a few minutes I asked partners to switch. Before the next five minutes were up, I channeled everyone to move from talking to writing, reminding them that they could act as their own Question Crew, answering questions as they revised. I added a new point to our anchor chart.

> **ANCHOR CHART**
>
> ### To Teach an Audience
>
> - Think, "Who is my audience?" and "What will they want to learn?"
> - Help readers picture the information.
>   - Add description.
>   - Add comparisons.
> - Hook readers with an interesting lead.
>   - Ask a question.
>   - Introduce the chapter's topic with pop-out words.
> - **Clear up confusion.**
>   - **Answer the readers' questions.**

You've now implicitly modeled two different ways to physically revise a chapter in this lesson. During the teaching, you added a sentence right onto the page where you had space. Now, you added a revision strip containing additional information. It's helpful to show kids how revision can look, reminding them of the options available.

By this point in the bend, kids will have worked with their regular partners long enough to become familiar with each other's work. By working with a new partner for a short time, kids will read each other's work with fresh eyes and identify even more confusing parts that need to be clarified.

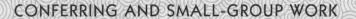

Supporting Writers as They Move through the Writing Process

YOUR MINILESSON TODAY encourages kids to reread their own writing, asking questions of it, and to revise their writing based on the questions they and their partner had asked. You'll probably find that your kids are eager to leave "Wow!" and "Huh?" Post-its and even add a word here or a sentence there throughout their pieces to answer those questions. You may need to remind them that writers often need to make larger-scale revisions to their work—especially when they need to clarify information for their audience. Adding in a small revision strip here and there will not do the trick! You'll also probably see that your writers need help to continue writing more chapters in their information books and to shift from writing one book to writing another. They'll also need to be reminded that their work today need not follow the minilesson, but rather can draw on all they have learned until now.

Help writers to use their time well, and teach them to make a plan for their work time.

You might take a moment today to observe how students get to work. You may notice that some writers open their folders, pull out their most recent book, and get back to the work they left off the day before. You may notice other writers who seem unsure how to begin, as they open their folders and just stare at the work inside. You may also notice, as you peek into kids' folders, that some writers have yet to move on to a second or third book in this bend.

After a minute of research, you might conduct a few table conferences. Perhaps you'll say to one table, "Writers, I have been watching you get started with your work today. Can I give you a little tip? Writers always plan for their time. It's just like recess! When you go out to recess, you plan what you are going to play and who you are going to play with, right? Well, when you write, you plan what you need to work on, and what tools will help you do that work." Signal for kids to start planning their work time right then and there. Be ready to offer some tips that will launch them into productive work. Perhaps they should recognize that their current book is done for now and they need to plan and start a whole new book. Maybe they need to revise several chapters with

the anchor chart close at hand, or add in a handful of new chapters to a book in progress. Be sure to have new booklets, pages, and copies of charts at hand to get writers started with the necessary tools and materials.

Support students in making large-scale revision.

Your second-graders often feel so proud to have accomplished something that they are reluctant, as most people are, to make any changes to their writing. As teachers, of course, we all know that at times students' writing can be confusing. Writing that needs clarification is often best fixed with large-scale revision, which requires kids to write those chapters again, incorporating big changes.

To get buy-in from your students, you may have to set up a more engaging and convincing scenario around revision. You might show these reluctant revisers how you make big revisions to your own writing. Gather them and say, "Writers, when you were in kindergarten you didn't know how to tie your shoes. Many of you could only wear Velcro sneakers. Then you learned how to tie your shoes and you abandoned your old Velcro sneakers for the lace-up kind. Writing is a bit like learning to tie your shoes. You write as best you can until you learn something new. Then your writing starts to change. You put your first draft down, pick up a new page, and write that part again in a new way."

Next, place your first draft of a chapter next to your revised one and invite writers to study them. Ask which one they would hope to pick up and read. You may even invite them to point out the ways in which you improved your writing after learning so much about writing for an audience. Of course, this work would also be effective if kids studied peer writing. Kids need to envision the before-and-after picture to buy into the idea that, yes, revision is worth it! After studying this example together, invite students to choose their own chapter to revise. Hand them a new page or two, and congratulate them on the fact that they are ready to grow as writers.

"Writers, eyes up here a minute." Once I had the class's attention, I said, "Earlier when you were rereading with a new partner, some kids had a different reason for going, 'Huh?' Some of you got confused by your partner's writing, not because that person's *information* was hard to understand, but because his or her *writing* was hard to read, with lots of misspelled words—even ones that are on the word wall!

"Thumbs up if you noticed this kind of writing confusion today in your own or your partner's writing!" Lots of thumbs went up.

"Here's the good news. This is an easy kind of confusion to fix! All it takes is a little time spent carefully rereading, checking that you spelled word wall words correctly.

"You could also reread and check that your sentences don't go on and on with lots of *ands* and that the punctuation makes sense. If you asked a question, did you use a question mark at the end? If you said something surprising, did you use an exclamation mark?

"Right now, take a minute to quickly check your writing for these things, and make sure to fix up any confusion. After you're done, swap writing with your partner to check that things make sense. I'll add this strategy to the chart."

ANCHOR CHART

To Teach an Audience

- Think, "Who is my audience?" and "What will they want to learn?"
- Help readers picture the information.
    - Add description.
    - Add comparisons.
- Hook readers with an interesting lead.
    - Ask a question.
    - Introduce the chapter's topic with pop-out words.
- Clear up confusion.
    - Answer the readers' questions.
    - **Fix spelling and punctuation mistakes.**

Clear up confusion

Answer questions
(Who?) (Where?) (Why?)

Fix spelling and Punctuation
(ponte) → pointy   Bakers can first up to 500 cupcakes in one day

You will, of course, want to have a repertoire of other ways to support large-scale revision at your fingertips. Encourage kids to reread and note places where they can turn a sentence into a paragraph, and then add in a revision strip to do so. You might remind kids that sometimes when writers reread their work, they realize that what they wrote as one chapter is actually two chapters—with both of the new bits being just the beginnings of chapters. These writers can take two new pages and begin two new chapters just like that! You can also channel kids to use the Information Writing Checklist or the anchor chart of the bend to remind them of ways that authors elaborate. Most importantly, if you listen spellbound to what writers have to say about a topic, and then encourage them to put that information on the page, they will find themselves adding on to chapters or even giving them another go.

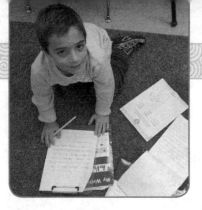

Showing Off Grown-Up Writing
Tackling First-Grade Strategies in Second-Grade Ways

Remind students of several familiar strategies for teaching their readers. Challenge them to use these strategies as they revise their writing.

"Writers, I went to my niece's skateboarding competition last week. It was so cool! People would show off their tricks, trying to outdo one another. They'd do a trick, then make it even more sophisticated, more grown-up—they'd say, 'Oh yeah? Well, now, look at *this*!' Well, you can do that, too! You can show off the tricks you have for teaching information. Now that you're second-graders, with lots of writing tricks up your sleeves, you can say, 'Now look at *this*!' and make your writing even more grown-up."

I pulled out the "Think About Questions" Post-it from earlier. "Ms. Bellino didn't just let me borrow this one strategy, she let me borrow the whole chart!"

I revealed the rest of the "How Can I Teach My Readers?" chart.

"You've already used this first-grade strategy, 'Think about Questions' in a *grown-up*, second-grade way. That made me think, could we say to this whole chart, to every strategy, 'Oh yeah? Now look at this!'?" I put my hands on my hips as I spoke, making myself look extra bossy.

"What if we have a *writing* competition to see if we can make our writing even more grown-up?

"Okay, let's make our writing even more grown-up and tell it, 'Now look at this!'" I invited kids to repeat the phrase along with me. Then I said, "Open to one of your chapters and reread the last line you wrote. Quickly, make it a twin sentence. You'll remember that means that if you have one sentence about something, you can write a second sentence with even more information." I pointed toward that strategy on the chart as the kids began writing furiously. "Who has done it?" Hands rose all around the carpet. "Yippee! Ready to tell those twin sentences, 'Now look at this!'?" The kids nodded. "This time, turn those twin sentences into *triplets*, or even *quadruplets*—teach more! Go ahead, make your writing grown-up!"

After a few moments, I called the class back together. "Right now, take a peek here." I pointed back toward the chart. "And pick another strategy you'd like to try out in a more grown-up way. When you have that strategy in mind, share your plan for turning a first-grade strategy into a second-grade strategy with the person next to you and then give it a try!"

Setting Goals to Make Nonfiction Books Better

AT THE TEACHERS COLLEGE READING AND WRITING PROJECT, we often suggest that teachers from different grades in a school convene and then, as a group, walk through a classroom at every grade level to glean a sense for how one topic is supported across the grade levels. One topic that teachers often select to study is revision. Imagine that a group of teachers went into a kindergarten in your school and studied revision for five minutes. One teacher might look at the charts and see evidence of teaching around revision. Another might look through a few kids' writing folders to note the revisions that kids seem apt to do. Another teacher might have the job to sit with one child, then another, and to ask, "If you *were* going to revise this piece, what *might* you do? How might that go exactly?"

Now imagine that group came to your classroom and took in whatever there was to see, looking at the different ways in which revision shows up in your classroom. What would they see? Would they see booklets revised with flaps and strips where leads had been written and rewritten or bits of elaboration had been added in? Or would they see mostly first-draft writing, untouched by revision save for that which had been specifically prompted by you within a conference or small group?

In all too many classrooms, the actual amount of revision is disappointing. Your hope should be that visitors to your room would not conclude that your second-graders revised only when you nudged them to do so. Today's session puts revision front and center. You'll remind your writers that they now know a lot about writing nonfiction books and what makes them ready for an audience. This means, of course, that they will want to revise their books in ways that get all parts and pages ready for their debut reading!

In today's minilesson, you'll invite writers to zoom in on certain parts of the Information Writing Checklist and work on one goal for writing from chapter to chapter across one book. You'll cut the checklist into tear-off flaps and encourage writers to choose a flap that will help make their book better for their reader. So if a student tears off the part of the checklist that says, "I tried to include words that show I'm an expert on the topic,"

IN THIS SESSION, you'll teach children that nonfiction writers set goals for work they can do to make a chapter even better. Then they transfer each goal from chapter to chapter, so that the whole book is ready to be read by others.

GETTING READY

✔ By the beginning of this session, students should have written two or three books. If they have not, you may wish to support their efforts to increase volume during conferring and small-group work.

✔ A marker to use as an imaginary microphone (see Connection)

✔ Your demonstration writing (see Teaching)

✔ A copy of the Information Writing Checklist for grades 1 and 2 for each child, with each strategy cut toward the center into flaps, plus one to display to the class (see Teaching, Active Engagement, and Share) ✧

✔ Student writing folders containing their most recent books (see Active Engagement)

✔ "To Teach an Audience" anchor chart, plus mini-versions for each child (see Link and Mid-Workshop Teaching) ✧

✔ Post-its for children to jot mini-reviews of each other's nonfiction books (see Share)

✔ A nonfiction book with a blurb on the back (see Share)

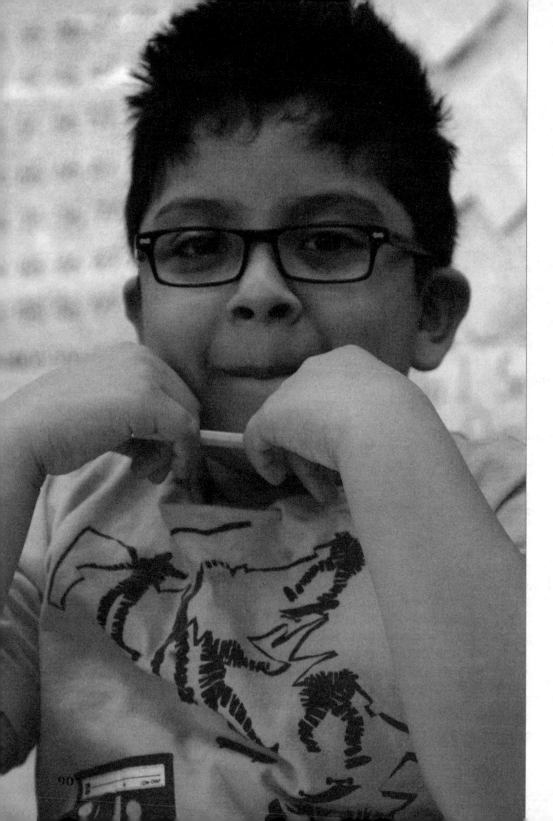

the student can hold that part of the checklist up to all parts of his book and check the sentences, headings, captions, and diagrams in each chapter for topic-specific vocabulary.

"Writers will want to revise in ways that get all parts and pages ready for their debut reading!"

The checklist will not be the only tool you'll invite writers to use across the session. Bring your anchor charts front and center! In the mid-workshop teaching, you'll remind writers that anchor charts can provide much needed support as students work to get their writing ready for others. In your conferring and small-group work, you might find it helpful to show writers how to look between their checklist goals and the work from the unit to make big and small changes to each chapter as they get their books ready for another celebration.

90

Setting Goals to Make Nonfiction Books Better

CONNECTION

Pretend to be a news reporter and quickly interview a few students about how they write to teach an audience.

As the class gathered on the rug, I prepared to take on the role of a newscaster. I walked across the room, grabbed my imaginary microphone (a marker), and walked back toward the rug. In my best newscaster voice, I announced, "Good morning! You are watching Room 203B News. I'm here today with the class of room 203B to answer the question that second-graders around the country and the globe have been asking, 'What do *you* need to do when you want to write to teach an audience?'"

The class giggled as I said, "We're lucky to have a whole class of kids who have the answers, right here with us today. Let's hear what they have to say."

I turned toward Margaret. "How would you answer this question? What is it that second-graders need to know about writing to teach an audience?" I held the "microphone" out.

"Well, you need to write what your readers want to know," Margaret replied, trying to be serious.

Pointing the "microphone" back toward me, I said, "Ah, yes, ladies and gents. You heard it here first! Teach an audience what they want to know!"

With that, the rest of the class's hands shot up. "Teddy, how do you write to teach your audience?" I asked, holding out the "microphone" to him.

"I write what stuff looks like," he said.

"Oh, yes! You add descriptions. Well, folks, it seems second-graders have good ideas about the age-old question: 'How do I write to teach an audience?' Signing off from Room 203B!"

Normally your connection wouldn't involve students sharing out information, as you want to keep this part of the minilesson brief. In this case, allowing a few writers to share out what they have learned so far as nonfiction writers not only helps get their juices flowing, but also allows you a moment to check in on their learning. Interview just a few kids so that the minilesson keeps moving!

Resume the role of teacher and announce that all of this knowledge means the class's books are nearly ready for the stage.

I set down my marker "microphone" to show the class that I was back in my role of teacher. "Class, it's clear from that newscast that you have learned quite a lot about writing to teach an audience—so much so that your books are almost 'onstage' ready!"

❖ **Name the teaching point.**

"Today I want to teach you that checklists and other reminders for ways to write well can be *way* more powerful than you think. Checklists and other reminders don't just give a tip for one thing you can do, one day, in one part. Instead, they remind you of work you can do over and over, page after page, day after day."

TEACHING

Remind children about how they have used the Information Writing Checklist to help identify goals, then tell them that there is a way to use the checklist to make their writing even better.

"Do you remember earlier in this unit, when I gave you each a copy of the Information Writing Checklist? You've been using it to check your writing, and when you checked 'Not Yet' for some of the things on the list, you turned those into goals to work on. And that's *so* important, because those goals help you know what you need to do to make your writing better and better!

"I saw many of you read a chapter and then read down the checklist to find one goal, fix up that one page, and then quickly find another goal to work on. That's a great start, but I want you to know those checklists can be even *more* helpful if you stick with one goal for longer, making sure you've met that goal page after page, chapter after chapter."

Share a comparison to show children that they can use strategies on the Information Writing Checklist to accomplish particular goals in their books, and then carry those goals across chapters.

"Have you ever seen a bulletin board, maybe at the supermarket or at the post office, that is filled with signs that say things like 'Car for sale' or 'Babysitter available'? At the bottom of each sign are lots of flaps that you can rip off, which describe the service or item offered. You look at the bulletin board, find a car, a babysitter, or whatever else is advertised, and grab the flap you need—just like that!"

Under the document camera, I placed a new version of the Information Writing Checklist, with each strategy cut toward the center, creating tearable flaps. I ruffled the flaps to show the class how I had cut up the checklist to make it look similar to a bulletin board advertisement.

"You can use your checklist in a similar way to set goals that you'll stick with for your entire book. Here's how. Just like when you've set goals before, you'll reread your chapter and then read down the checklist, finding places you have

John Hattie's research has found that disconfirmation is more valuable than confirmation when learning something new. Feedback that disconfirms requires a learner to make a change and, in turn, supports retrieval of that information in the future. If a child's response does not match the question asked, you could respond with disconfirming feedback by saying, "I heard you say . . . Am I right? If so, that doesn't match what we've learned. Could you check the chart and revise your idea?"

to check 'Not Yet.' When you find a goal to work on, rip off that flap, the one that your chapter needs, just like that!" I ripped off a flap for dramatic effect.

I placed my bakery book under the document camera. "Once you have chosen a goal flap, you'll use it to make that page better, just like you've done before." I laid the flap on the first page of my book. "But then, you'll transfer that goal, take it with you from page to page, making each page, each chapter even better!" I started flipping slowly through the pages of my bakery book with one hand, holding my goal flap in the other, and laying the goal on each page to show how I could take that goal from page to page.

ACTIVE ENGAGEMENT

Set kids up to try this work, using their own checklists. As they review their writing and choose goals, circulate and guide their choices as needed. Then get them started revising, goal in hand.

"It looks like you're all ready for your own 'bulletin board' checklist. Great!" I passed out checklists, already cut into flaps, to the class, and prompted kids to starting reading down the checklist as they waited for their classmates to all have the tool in hand.

"Writers, put your book on your lap. Start rereading your first chapter and think, 'How can I make this chapter better?' Then look down at your checklist, and search carefully for the flap that will help make that chapter—really your whole book—even better. Get started!" I circulated.

After a few seconds, I paused writers, saying, "Now that most of you have chosen a goal flap, it's time to start the important work of making that chapter, and then each of the other chapters in your book, better than before! Remember to take your first goal from one page to another. Get started."

As the class worked, I looked for kids to be turning pages and physically taking their goal flap with them. I circulated, complimenting writers who used their goal in multiple places. "Sara, you didn't just include definitions on one page. You are working so hard to include definitions on every page! Yes!"

LINK

Remind children of the importance of goal-setting. Encourage them to do the same work across their books, using other goals from the checklist, once they've finished the first.

I gathered the class once more. "Writers, I know you've only *just* gotten started, but I wanted to remind you how important the work of goal-setting is. You each have a bulletin board checklist, filled with lots of potential goals that will make your writing ready for your audience.

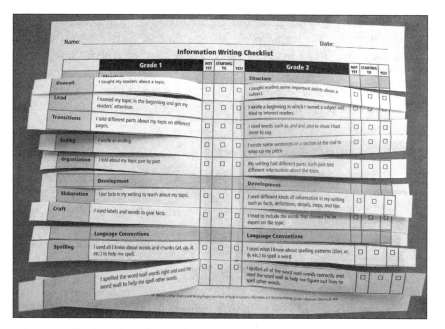

FIG. 11–1   A "bulletin board" checklist made by cutting each goal into tearable flaps.

The point of today's session is not for you to choose the part of the checklist you think is important for each writer, but rather for kids to self-assess and reflect on their work to make their own decisions. If writers seem unsure about which part of the checklist to choose, help them make a quick decision here at the meeting area. Then make a mental note to check in on those writers during your conferring today.

"Once you use one goal to improve each page, each chapter, your work isn't finished. Next you'll reread your checklist thinking, 'How *else* can I make this chapter and this *book* better for my reader?' Grab another flap and take it from page to page again, fixing up your whole book with that goal in mind." Children nodded, eager to get back to work.

"Okay, writers. Either stay here on the rug to keep working, or head back to your tables. Your choice!" I added the new goal-setting strategy to the anchor chart.

ANCHOR CHART

To Teach an Audience

- Think, "Who is my audience?" and "What will they want to learn?"
- Help readers picture the information.
  - Add description.
  - Add comparisons.
- Hook readers with an interesting lead.
  - Ask a question.
  - Introduce the chapter's topic with pop-out words.
- Clear up confusion.
  - Answer the readers' questions.
  - Fix spelling and punctuation mistakes.
- **Set goals and meet them page after page.**

Set goals and meet them page after page

Research by Mihaly Csikszentmihalyi suggests that when a person is completely immersed in an activity, he or she can experience an energized and pure state of joy that Csikszentmihalyi calls flow. *When you give children only a brief moment to begin working in the meeting space during the minilesson, you might then also give them the opportunity to remain working in the meeting space so that you don't disrupt their flow.*

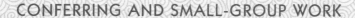
Fostering Self-Assessment, Goal-Setting, and Revision

TODAY YOUR STUDENTS are using specific goals from the Information Writing Checklist to drive their revision work. You might begin today with quick table conferences to make sure writers are up and running with their revision work. Your students have used the checklist before, so your work today will be less about clarifying language of the checklist and more about helping students use the checklist effectively. Your goal is to help students become more independent with self-assessment.

(continues)

Name Emilia   Date
Diffrent Kinds

ta-ta-ta-ta-ta-ta-ta-ta whats that sound?ta-ta-ta-ta-ta-ta. Can it be?ta-ta-ta-ta-ta-ta-ta.Is it true? ta-ta-ta-ta-ta-ta.Is it a bunny? ta-ta-ta-ta-ta-ta ta. Yes it is. Yeah!

It ▮▮▮▮ss the yard whon ▮▮▮▮ny's can be

> I wrote a beginning in which I named a subject and tried to interest readers.   ☐ ☐ ☐

not say-ing ▮▮▮▮ Pink though. I'm ▮▮▮▮ can be black, tan, ▮▮▮▮ beige.There are many diffrent kinds of bunny's some are spotted, striped and two diffrent colors that just flow into each other.Now some People think hares are rabbits but they are just in the rabbit family.

Name _____   Date _____
Diet

NIBB-LE! CHOMP! CRUNCH! Look theres a bunny eating some grass. over there! Lets feed it!

Wait! You can't just feed a bunny anything.Most bunny's eat carrots and grass.Some bunny's might eat wheat but some don't.A rabbit may eat diffrent kinds of plants most of them drink either milk or water. Some eat honey but to much honey is not good for them. So, for a treat you Should dip a stich into a jar of honey, just once not twice and then put the stick in the cage.

FIG. 11–2   Emilia chose the goal flap for leads. She revised the beginning of each chapter so that her first sentences would interest her readers.

Help writers apply their goals to each chapter.

At first glance, some sections of the checklist may seem to fit only with certain parts of an information text. For example, in Bend I, you told writers that information texts begin with leads that get readers interested in the topic. You also taught writers that information texts end in ways that keep readers thinking. Now, you can remind writers that each part of the checklist can be used to improve each chapter.

Perhaps you notice a writer is working on the "Overall" section of the checklist as a goal. This part asks writers to teach "some important points about the subject." The child might be leafing through her book to see if she has all the important points of her topic in her piece. This is fine, but today's minilesson invited writers to check each *chapter* for important points. You may support writers with this work in one-to-one conferences, or you could extend this work to the whole table and say, "Writers, I was just talking to Lily about how she can use her goal to improve not just her book, but also each of her chapters. She chose the goal of teaching important points about her topic. She knows that across her whole book she will teach important points about her topic—these will be her chapters—but what she just realized was that each *chapter* should also have important points. That way, her audience will also learn about the most important pieces of information in her subtopics." Then you could invite everyone to give this a go. "Could all of you look at your goals right now and think, 'How can I use my goal to make each *chapter* better?' When you think you have an idea, turn and tell the person next to you." Listen in to their ideas, voicing over tips for different checklist goals. Then, encourage writers to get to work making each chapter the best it can be using their individual goals. Your writers will have written a bunch of books by now within this unit, so be sure to encourage them to revise and edit more than one of those books.

Help writers make connections between checklist and mentor texts.

The writing checklist gives readers goals, but doesn't give them strategies. Your teaching can help them with the "how-to" part of meeting a goal. One way is to encourage the student to study a mentor text that accomplishes the work he wants to do. For example, if the writer wants to fix up transitions, he can notice the transitions in a mentor text. You will probably want to help the writer locate appropriate mentor texts that illustrate whatever it is the checklist has channeled the child to try. You could suggest that, just like they learned in Bend I, writers think about nonfiction texts they have been reading. Encourage them to choose texts that do the work they are aiming to do as a writer.

You may come across a few writers who need guidance selecting appropriate goals. A writer who obsesses about each and every word's spelling may need help with elaboration as well as spelling, and you may need to rally the writer to embrace that goal.

MID-WORKSHOP TEACHING
Using the Anchor Chart to Set More Goals

"Writers, I want to remind you that while you're getting your books ready for readers, you might also refer to our anchor chart." I pointed at the chart and said, "I've made small copies of it, so if any of you want to use it to steer your revisions, come and get one of these tiny copies. You can keep the chart at your elbow and use it almost as a to-do list.

"You'll want to make sure that you've tried these strategies not just in *one* place, but in lots of places. Maybe even in every chapter! Just like you use the checklist, you can read down the chart and find a strategy you haven't tried, or one you haven't tried in *lots* of places. You might jot it on a Post-it so you can stick the reminder beside you as you work from chapter to chapter. Alright, back to work!"

Writing Reviews Using the Checklist and the Anchor Chart

Invite children to draw on their persuasive writing skills, the Information Writing Checklist, and the anchor chart to write mini-reviews of their partner's book.

"Writers, bring your nonfiction book, Post-its, and checklist—including the flaps you ripped off to use—with you to the meeting area." Once the class was gathered, I said, "Writers, soon you are going to put your own nonfiction books in the library. I've been thinking . . . do you remember that in first grade, when you studied review writing, you wrote reviews of books? You gave your opinion, and then lots of reasons, to convince people to read books that you love.

"I wonder, could you use those same persuasive skills to write mini-reviews of each other's books?" I held up a book and pointed to a review blurb on the back. "These small reviews could live on the back of your partner's book. That way, your audience will know all of the reasons why they should give that book a read."

"Yeah!" kids called out, excited by this idea.

"Great! Since you've been using the checklist and the anchor chart, your *reasons* can come straight from them! If your partner," I pointed to the checklist and read, "'wrote a beginning in which he or she tried to interest readers,' that might be one reason you use to convince an audience to read your partner's book." I pointed back at the chart. "Hmm, . . . what could some other reasons in a review be . . . ?" Children read down the chart, calling out options that they could use as reasons in a book review.

Channel children to switch books with their partner and to write a review of their partner's book on Post-its. As they do this work, circulate, offering praise and tips.

"Wow! Listen to all of those reasons to read nonfiction books. Now, in a moment, you'll switch books with your partner. You'll read your partner's book, using the checklist and the chart to find some things that your partner did well! Then, you can use Post-its to leave a mini-review for your partner's audience. Switch and start reviewing!" I circulated the meeting area, marveling at the students' reviews of each other's books and prompting them to look at the chart and checklist for more reasons for their reviews.

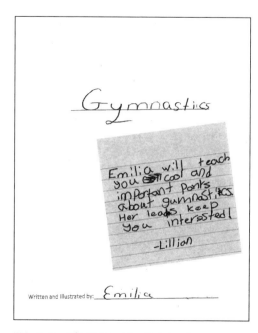

FIG. 11–3 Lily reviews Emilia's book on gymnastics using the Information Writing Checklist for ideas.

Session 12

Editing Nonfiction Writing

Fixing Up Spelling Mistakes for Readers

IN THIS SESSION, you'll teach children that writers draw on strategies they know to fix up their writing for readers, making sure it is easy to read.

GETTING READY

- ✔ A white board and a marker for each child (see Connection, Active Engagement, and Conferring and Small-Group Work)
- ✔ The Language Conventions strand of the Information Writing Checklist, grades 1 and 2, to display to the class (see Connection and Link)
- ✔ "Use the Words You Know to Help You Spell Hard Words" chart (see Teaching)
- ✔ Writing by a second-grader who is not in your class with some of the same types of spelling mistakes your writers make (see Teaching and Confer and Small-Group Work)

AS YOU NEAR THE END OF THIS BEND, take a step back and notice how your writers have grown. Look between their writing from the start of this unit and the writing they are doing now. Perhaps they write with greater volume and stamina or try new writing moves. Maybe some look to published nonfiction texts, flagging craft moves they want to try, and then trying those same moves in their own books.

In the midst of all this big work, you won't want to forget the "little" work that will make the difference between a readable book and one that is less audience-friendly. The last session invited writers to revise their books—to use parts of the checklist to guide revisions, big and small. Today's work will channel them to look at their writing through the lens of editing, making sure each chapter, and book, is readable.

Before teaching this session, take a look at your most recent assessment of your children's spelling patterns and note the patterns that your students use and confuse, as well as ones they have yet to learn. Which students need to learn to break words into syllables? Which need to learn to use parts of words to spell new words? If students experienced *Lessons from the Masters*, the first unit in the Units of Study in Opinion, Information, and Narrative Writing series, be sure to remind them to draw on the work they learned to do in that unit.

Today you will invite writers to assume the role of editor and to use their word study tools and strategies to fix up words. In the mid-workshop, you will remind them that they need to edit all parts of their books including their headings and captions, not just the sentences. To prepare for today's editing work, you may want to place tools, such as charts and white editing tape, at each table. In the share, partners will support each other as they've been doing across the bend, working with an eye, and ear, toward editing.

Tomorrow students will celebrate all of their writing efforts thus far, so today you'll encourage them to work hard to make sure each word of each book is ready for an audience to read!

Editing Nonfiction Writing
Fixing Up Spelling Mistakes for Readers

CONNECTION

Tell children that before they share their books with an audience, the books must be easy to read. Highlight the importance of making sure an audience can read a book without the author's help.

"Writers and editors, you'll not only need your writing folders in the meeting area today; you will also need a white board and a marker." I waited a few moments for the children to settle.

"You are just one day away from giving out books to your audience. You have worked hard to make sure your books are chock full of interesting information! But . . ." I leaned in. "Before you can share your books with an audience, you need to make sure they are easy to read!"

I displayed the Language Conventions strand of the Information Writing Checklist under the document camera. "*Some of you used this part of the checklist yesterday, transferring editing strategies from chapter to chapter.*" I looked around the room and saw that only a few heads nodded.

❖ **Name the teaching point.**

"Today I want to remind you that writers make sure their writing is easy to read. One way you can do this is by using your knowledge of words you know how to spell to help you fix up misspelled words or to spell brand-new words."

TEACHING

Remind students of kindergarten, when they had to stretch out each word. Highlight growth, naming that students now have a large bank of words that they can spell with automaticity.

"Writers, quickly think all the way back to kindergarten. Can you remember the days when you needed to pause before every single word you wrote, saying it s-l-o-w-l-y out loud over and over to listen for and record each sound?" The students looked around and nodded, agreeing that they remembered.

◆ COACHING

Connecting one day's teaching to the next helps writers understand that each day's lesson stands on the shoulders of the ones that came before it.

Use the words You Know to Help You Spell Hard words

1. Think of a word you know how to spell that is sort of like the hard word.

strange   sideways

2. Ask, "How are they the same?"

3. Use ways the two words are the same to help you decide how to spell the hard word.

"Now you don't need to pause before every single word. Your pencils fly across the pages of your books. That's because the piggybank inside your brain that's full of words you know how to spell has grown! The more you read and the more you write, the more words you learn! There are hundreds, maybe thousands of words that you know how to spell without even giving it a thought."

Tell kids that they can draw on their spelling knowledge to figure out how to spell new and tricky words. Demonstrate how to do that with a piece of writing from another second-grader.

"Here's the thing. When you are editing your writing, you can use your bank of words to help you fix up words that are misspelled. Even if a word isn't in that bank of 'Known Words,' there are words you *do* know how to spell that can help you spell words you don't yet know how to spell. Here's what you do," I said, as I pointed to the "Use the Words You Know to Help You Spell Hard Words" one-day chart.

"Start by thinking of a word in your 'I know it' list that has a part that is the same as the word you are stuck on. Then think about that word you know and ask yourself, 'How are they the same?' Then, use ways the two words are the same to help you decide how to spell the hard word.

"Another second-grader, Gracie, needs your help editing her writing." I put a piece of second-grade writing up under the document camera.

"I was reading through Gracie's writing and look! This word *strange* is not easy to read here. It took me a while to figure out what it said. Do you agree?" I pointed to the word *schange* to show the class and they nodded.

"Hmm, . . . well let's see. What words are on my 'I know it' list that could help me spell *strange*?" I paused, leaving time for them to think. Kids in the class started eagerly waving their hands to share, and I signaled for them to hold onto their thoughts. "Oh, I've got it! *Strange* sounds a bit like *strong*. And guess what, *strong* is a word that I know how to spell."

I pointed to Step 2 on the chart. "So now, let me think, 'How are they the same?'" I said *strange* and *strong* out loud, modeling to listen for parts of words that are similar. "Well, the beginning of both words sounds the same, so I'm thinking that I should use what I know about how the word *strong* starts to spell the word *strange*."

I pointed to Step 3 to signal that I was moving down each step of the chart and then I quickly jotted *strong* on a white board and held it up. "Here is *strong*. It seems like *str-* is that part that sounds the same as *strange*." I then wrote *strange* underneath *strong*, showing the class how I used the same beginning blend for both.

It's important that as kids grow as readers and writers, their strategies for decoding and encoding grow as well. By contrasting your second-grader's earlier strategy of stretching each word, to record each sound, with the more sophisticated strategy taught today, of using word parts, you signal to students this growth.

Writers need to use instruction in spelling patterns and encoding strategies to be most effective when they spell new words. Today's teaching shines a spotlight on both!

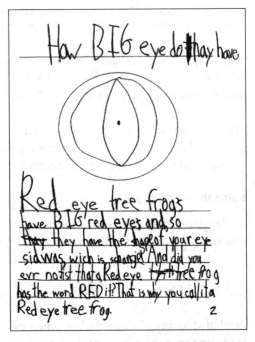

FIG. 12–1 A page from Gracie's chapter about red-eyed tree frogs contains spelling errors that can be fixed using today's teaching.

ACTIVE ENGAGEMENT

Invite partners to continue reading the chapter, circling in the air any misspelled words that need to be fixed up.

"Writers, now it's your turn to try. Quickly, put on your editor's cap and get your white board and marker ready!" The class placed imaginary caps on their heads and got their materials ready.

"With your partner, read Gracie's writing and use your finger to circle in the air any words that you think need an editor—words that Gracie needs to make sure are easy to read." As partnerships read the chapter, I crouched down near them and recorded the words I saw them "circling."

Share out what children noticed. Invite partners to choose a strategy to help them fix up a misspelled word.

"Wow, editors, you circled a whole bunch of words. Many of you circled the words *sideways*. Put a thumb up if you did." Kids lifted their thumbs to signal that they had noticed the misspelled word.

"Editors, work together to think, 'Is there a word that I already know how to spell that can help me fix this word up?' You can use a word from the word wall or a word from the bank of words in your brain. You'll then think how the two words are the same and use that word to spell the misspelled word."

Voice over the strategies you see partners using.

As kids got to work, I voiced over the words they knew and how they were using them to fix up misspelled words. "Iris is using the word *always* from the word wall to fix up the word *sideways*. They end the same way. Matthew is using the word *hide* to fix up *side-* in *sideways*." I held up his white board to show kids who looked over. "He knows that *hide* and *side* sound the same at the end, so that they could end the same way."

LINK

Send students off to edit with a reminder to use words they already know to help them spell new words. Remind them how the checklist can help them correct spelling and punctuation mistakes.

"Editors, spelling new words or fixing up misspelled words can sometimes feel tricky, but it doesn't have to. When you head off to edit the books inside of your folder, remember to use words you already know—from inside your brain, from the word wall, and even from around the classroom—to spell words that are new."

Reiterating the steps is helpful as students combine both a process and strategies! Use this time in the active engagement to observe how students take on the work of editing for spelling. This will help inform your conferring and small-group work later.

Note that anything you teach your second-graders can be incorporated in not just the children's most recent book but all the information books they have written up to that point.

"You each have two, maybe even three books inside of your folder. That means you have a lot of editing work to do to make each of the books easy for your audience to read." I quickly, once again, displayed the Language Conventions strand of the Information Writing Checklist. "You have choices to make. You can make your writing easy to read by fixing up misspelled words, but remember to use this part of the checklist to not only edit spelling errors, but to fix up punctuation as well. This is the part of the checklist that will help you make your writing easy to read. Remember to use it! Off you go, editors."

It's important to reiterate that editing isn't only fixing up spelling. Your writers will undoubtedly have a variety of ways they need to fix up their writing, from spelling to end punctuation to finding missing words.

Transferring Word Study Work and Spelling Strategies into Writing

I F ONE OF YOUR GOALS TODAY is to help students transfer word study work into writing, you can work toward that goal by taking the tools you use in word study time and making them available to students during writing workshop. Perhaps your class has a special chart that reminds students of the difference between long and short vowel sounds or the variety of vowel teams. Make sure those tools are accessible to students as they write. Many teachers find it helpful to keep extra copies in their writing centers.

To support students with more effective spelling strategies, you might want to start by comparing the spelling strategies your writers do use with some strategies that we have found particularly effective for second-grade writers. In addition to helping writers learn to use parts of one word to help them spell another word you might teach writers to clap syllables and then to write the word syllable by syllable, knowing that in each syllable there should be a vowel. It may also benefit some students to learn to try a word three ways and then study all three attempts, noticing the try that seems closest to what they think the word looks like in books. By this time in second grade, students will have a bank of vowel teams they are learning about in word study, so you may decide to bring that aspect of spelling front and center and invite writers to try out different vowel teams as they spell. Each strategy allows students to build on their knowledge of spelling patterns or other resources in the room.

Small-group interactive writing can be especially helpful for students who need to learn, practice, and internalize these strategies. Of course kids will need more than one interactive writing session before they start to take these strategies on as their own.

(continues)

MID-WORKSHOP TEACHING   Writers Edit Repeating Words

"Writers, I noticed that you aren't just looking to fix the spelling of words in your sentences. You're also remembering to fix words in your text features—in your diagrams, captions, and headings! Bravo! It's important to make *all* of your writing easy to read.

"Can I give you a quick tip? Writers sometimes use the same words in their sentences as they do in their text features. So if you fixed a word in one place—if you worked to spell it the best you could using all you know about how words work in a sentence—then take the time to fix it in other places, too!

"Right now, choose a word you fixed already today. Put your finger on it and take a good look at it. Now take that word with you as you reread the rest of your page and other pages to see if you need to fix that word anywhere else."

FIG.12–2   Lucas edits his chapter for spelling using a strategy chart.

When you gather a small group of three to five students for interactive writing, start by giving them white boards and dry erase markers. Get a page of writing from a kid in another class with some of the same types of spelling mistakes your writers in the small group make or create some sample writing that includes similar mistakes. Begin by telling children that this writer needs some extra support making his writing easy to read. "Writers, if you want to be sure your audience can learn from your book, you need to make sure your writing is easy to read." Reread the page and ask students to help you find words that need another look. Circle three to five words—you don't want too many—and remind writers of the strategies they already know by showing them the chart for spelling tricky words. You might say, "Writers, as we help this student edit his spelling, let's make sure we use strategies that will be helpful."

Perhaps one of the words you circled was *vehicle*. Students might start out by clapping the syllables, paying attention to the vowel sounds in each of the first two parts. Then for the ending you could encourage students to think about another word that has the same ending sound—perhaps *circle*. Working through a word in this way helps writers practice being flexible with a repertoire of strategies.

As you move from editing one word to editing another, take away your scaffold in increments by asking writers to identify the strategies that would be most helpful. You will want to leave the last word for them to edit on their own so that you're freed up to notice the ways in which they are working. This is helpful data for the next time you meet with them!

Partners Prepare for Publication
Catching Final Spelling and Punctuation Errors

Direct students to select one book to publish. Set partners up to read their writing and share feedback around spelling and convention errors.

I stood in the middle of the room and called for attention, "Writers, today we won't gather at the meeting area. Instead, could you first look through your books and pick the one you want to publish? Once you've chosen a book, meet with your partner. Find a spot to sit together and make sure you're not too close to another partnership."

As each partnership got together and settled into a spot I continued, "Your books are getting closer and closer to being ready for an audience. Now that you've chosen which book you will ready for its 'onstage' debut, I was thinking you would want some feedback from your practice audience. You could read your books aloud, making sure that you have the right punctuation in the right spots and that words are spelled correctly. As you're reading or listening, if you hear any bumps along the way, those will be places to check!

"Give me a thumbs up when you're ready to begin." When I saw all thumbs in the air, I said, "Partner 1, will you turn to a chapter you worked especially hard on today—one where you definitely made some changes? Draw a 'stage' around your spot. With your best author voice, read your chapter out loud to your audience—your partner.

"Partner 2, you have a big job. You will listen to how Partner 1's chapter sounds. If there are any bumpy or tricky spots, take a look at the chapter together. See if there's something you could change to make it better. Maybe there's missing punctuation or a word that still needs to be fixed. Ready, set, rehearse!"

Reading writing out loud not only allows students to hear places where information is confusing or sentences that need to be revised, it also helps them to see and hear places in their writing that are conventionally incorrect. Even though we expect that a piece of second-grade writing will have punctuation and spelling errors, reading aloud with a partner, a second set of eyes, allows writers to find errors to edit with greater ease.

Fancying Up Nonfiction Books for an Audience
Adding Final Touches

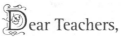

Dear Teachers,

Today is a day for celebration, because it marks the end of the second bend in this unit. In place of a full plan for the day, this letter presents a possibility for some instructional fanfare around the occasion.

There isn't a one of us who doesn't know that special rush one gets in those final moments, when weeks of preparation are brought to culmination. We feel that rush when the Thanksgiving dinner has been cooked, the bird lifted onto the platter and now there are just a few minutes before rounding up all the guests. In those last few minutes, a million jobs are done: the butter needs to get put on the table, the cranberry sauce, the jug of water.

Always, in those last moments, there is a flurry of urgency, and a kind of excitement that fuels extra-fast repairs. And always, we find ourselves anticipating the audience's response and making adjustments so that the work is greeted with exclamations of appreciation. You will try to create that same aura for all of your kids today, helping them to approach the final moments before their writers' celebration with rising spirits and high anticipation.

That is, we suggest you plan this session so that it provides your writers with an opportunity for a final rehearsal of their books before they reach their audience. During the minilesson, you may decide to study ways published authors prepare their books for readers—studying the details that make nonfiction books fun and enticing—and then give your writers time to fancy up and prepare their own books. Then, to celebrate, you could invite writers to become a "book fairy" to their intended reader by wrapping up a photocopy of one of their books as a gift (of course writers may choose to publish more than one of their books from this bend). Alternatively, you might celebrate by placing books in the classroom library, making a big deal of the occasion. Now that your class has written for an audience, their books belong next to the books written by Seymour Simon and Gail Gibbons. Of course, you and your students may have other ways to prepare and launch books out into the world. Your students have worked hard to write in ways that will help others enjoy learning about their topics, and now it's time to celebrate!

MINILESSON

In your connection, you may want to congratulate writers on making it this far and getting their books so close to being ready for an audience. You could say, "Writers, when you were in kindergarten, when it came time to publish your writing, you guys used an expression that I wonder if you remember still. You said, 'We gotta fix up and fancy up our writing.' And you know what? Those words are just perfect. They say exactly what writers do to get ready to publish a book. Writers fix up and fancy up their writing."

You could then name the teaching point. "Today I want to remind you that writers can look at published books to get ideas for their own books. Writers can notice the ways published authors fancy up their books for readers and try some of those same moves in their books, too."

As you move into the teaching, you might study published books by placing one mentor at a time under the document camera, studying the cover, the pictures, and the back of the book while you name ways that the authors made their books look fancy. Alternatively, you might divide the kids into four groups in the meeting space, placing a few published books with each group of children. You could coach each group as they study these books and write down what they notice on Post-its to collect for a one-day chart on fancying up nonfiction books. Children might notice things like the illustrations on the cover, a catchy title, or back cover blurbs. They might also notice the detailed, brightly colored illustrations and/or photographs inside the books, or an "about the author" page.

For the active engagement, you might have students look through another second-grader's book (a fictional second-grader) and make decisions about what that writer could do to fancy up his writing. You could say, "Writers, now that we know how authors fancy up their books, could you help this one neighbor of mine, BoBo, who has a draft that he wants to fix up and fancy up? Maybe you could help BoBo get his writing into shape?" You might then display BoBo's writing under the document camera, having the class use the chart to make plans for fancying up BoBo's writing. When a writer suggests that there could be an "about the author" page, for example, be sure you imagine how it might go, because of course the real purpose of this work is to help kids imagine what they can do to fancy up their own writing.

During your link, you might remind writers that they can always go back to published nonfiction texts as they work. Writers can study both what makes these books fancy and how authors did this work. Encourage writers to also think about their choices and what will capture their audience's interest.

CONFERRING AND SMALL-GROUP WORK

As you confer with writers, you may gather a group to study how to make meaningful decisions as they fancy up their books. You might turn back to the mentor texts you used during the minilesson, noticing how those authors are purposeful—how the ways they fancy up their books help those books teach more information. You could guide your students as they study illustrations, noticing how authors make sure the color, shape, and size of their illustrations help teach the audience. In books with photographs, you could show them how to use magnifying glasses to zoom in on the smaller details while you channel them to ponder how they could include some of those small details in their own books. Alternatively, you could choose

to study titles, both of books and of chapters. You might choose a variety of texts to study, noticing how some authors use puns or jokes to title their books and chapters while others use catchy words or phrases.

Whether you choose to study illustrations or titles with your students, make sure to give them a chance to transfer what they noticed into their own books as they get them ready for their audience.

Mid-Workshop Teaching

For your mid-workshop teaching, you could have students do a final check of their books. You might remind writers of all of the ways they've worked to get their books ready—using the checklist, using the anchor chart, and editing. It's possible that over the past few days your writers started revising or editing and did not finish when workshop ended. You could say, "Writers, you'll soon give your books to their intended audience, so it may be helpful to do a final check. You might look carefully through each part of your book to make sure it teaches, to make sure it's easy to read, to make sure it's fancy."

SHARE

During today's share, a mini-celebration, you will have the chance to recognize the progress your writers have made and to give them the experience of having their writing reach their intended audience. After all, they have worked hard to craft books for a specific person or group. You might, for example, decide that for this celebration the class will become "book fairies"! If you're using Units of Study for Teaching Reading for reading workshop, your children will have already had the experience of receiving books from a book fairy, but even if they have not, they will easily understand that this is a twist on the familiar role of tooth fairy. You could tell the class that they will become book fairies themselves, and will leave a photocopy of their book for their intended audience—making sure not to be caught! You could bring in wrapping paper and ribbons for children to wrap their book copies. Then you might suggest that authors write a note to attach to the package, describing why their audience will love the book inside the package.

Then again, you could ask each member of the class to place a photocopy of their book into the classroom library, into a container that holds nonfiction books. Your students can read the topics on the outside of the nonfiction bins and decide which bin should house their nonfiction book. You could also continue filling that bin labeled "Class 203B Authors" that you created for the beginning of this unit. Consider the excitement as kids place their books in your very own classroom library, waiting to be read by their peers. You might plan some reading time so that the class has the opportunity to read each other's books.

These are only two options, and of course you might think of other ones that will be special for your class. The important part of today is giving the class the opportunity to do something special with their books, giving their writing the "onstage" performance you have been promising all along!

Best of luck,
Valerie and Jen

Snakes!

look out!

max (my brother)

Written and Illustrated by: zoe

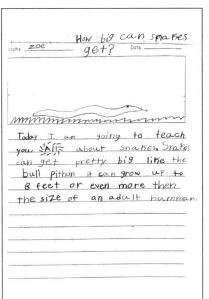

How big can snakes get?

Name zoe   Date

Today I am going to teach you All about snakes. Snakes can get pretty big like the bull pithon it can grow up to 8 feet or even more then the size of an adult humman.

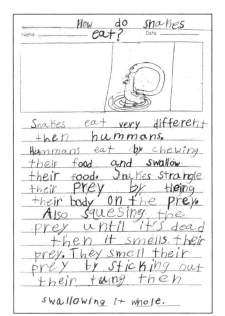

How do snakes eat?

Name   Date

Snakes eat very different then hummans. Hummans eat by chewing their food and swallow their food. Snakes strangle their prey by tieing their body on the prey. Also squesing the prey until it's dead then it smells their prey. They smell their prey by sticking out their tung then

swallowing it whole.

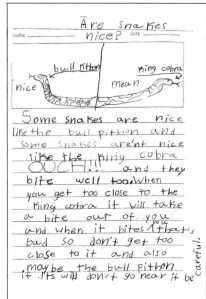

Are snakes nice?

Name   Date

bull pithon   king cobra

nice   mean

Some snakes are nice like the bull pithon and some snakes are'nt nice like the king cobra OUCH!!! and they bite well too. When you get too close to the king cobra it will take a bite out of you and when it bites you that's bad so don't get too close to it and also maybe the bull pithon if it's wild don't go near it be careful.

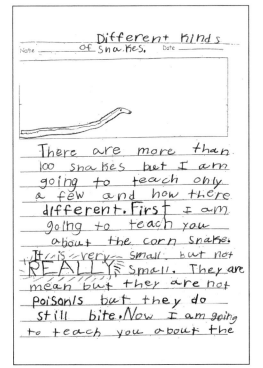

Different kinds of snakes.

Name   Date

There are more than 100 snakes but I am going to teach only a few and how there different. First I am going to teach you about the corn snake. It is very small but not REALLY small. They are mean but they are not poisonis but they do still bite. Now I am going to teach you about the

---

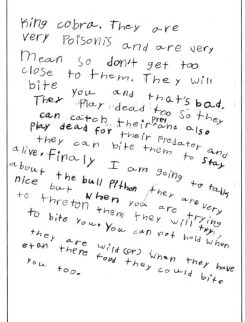

king cobra. They are very poisonis and are very mean so don't get too close to them. They will bite you and that's bad. They play dead too so they can catch their prey and also play dead for their predator and they can bite them to stay alive. Finaly I am going to talk about the bull pithon they are very nice but when you are trying to threton them they will try to bite you. You can not hold when they are wild (or) when they have eatan there food they could bite you too.

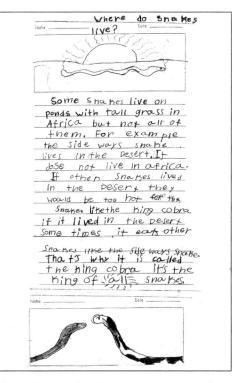

Where do snakes live?

Name   Date

Some snakes live on ponds with tall grass in Africa but not all of them. For example the side ways snake lives in the desert. It dose not live in africa. If other snakes lived in the desert they would be too hot for the snakes. Like the king cobra if it lived in the desert some times it eats other

snakes like the side ways snake. That's why it is called the king cobra it's the king of all snakes.

Name   Date

FIG. 13–1   Zoe wrote her book about snakes for her brother Max. She worked to engage her audience through catchy leads, descriptions, and advice.

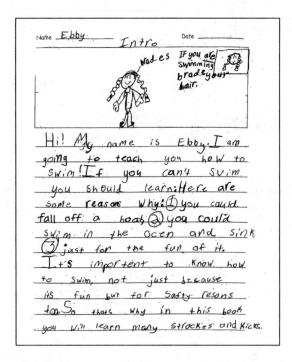

Name Ebby   Intro   Date ___

Hi! My name is Ebby. I am going to teach you how to swim! If you can't swim you should learn. Here are some reasons why: ① you could fall off a boat ② you could swim in the ocen and sink ③ just for the fun of it. It's important to know how to swim, not just because its fun but for safty resons too. So thats why in this book you will learn many strockes and kicks.

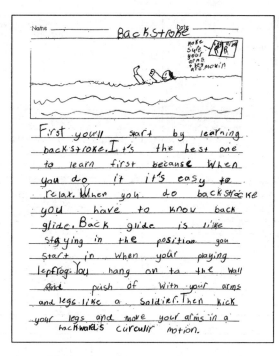

Name ___   Backstroke   Date ___

First you'll start by learning backstroke. It's the best one to learn first because when you do it it's easy to relax. When you do backstroke you have to know back glide. Back glide is like staying in the position you start in when your playing lepfrog. You hang on to the wall and push of with your arms and legs like a soldier. Then kick your legs and move your arms in a backwards curculir motion.

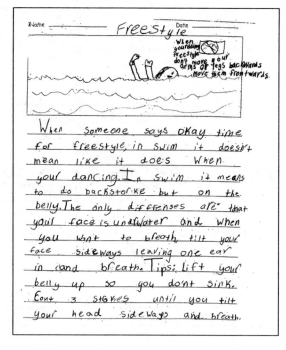

Name ___   Freestyle   Date ___

When someone says okay time for freestyle, in swim it doesn't mean like it does when your dancing. In swim it means to do backstroke but on the belly. The only diffrenses are that your face is underwater and when you want to breath tilt your face sideways leaving one ear in and breath. Tips: lift your belly up so you don't sink. Cont 3 strokes until you tilt your head sideways and breath.

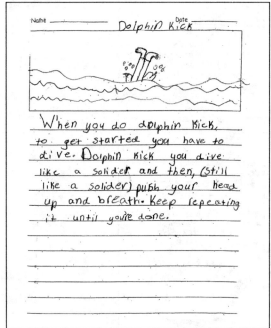

Name ___   Dolphin Kick   Date ___

When you do dolphin kick, to get started you have to dive. Dolphin kick you dive like a solider and then, (still like a solider) push your head up and breath. Keep repeating it until you're done.

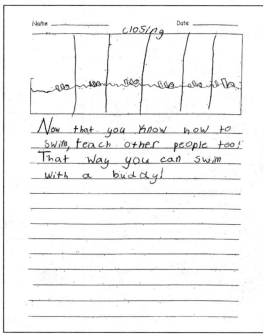

Name ___   closing   Date ___

Now that you know how to swim, teach other people too! That way you can swim with a buddy!

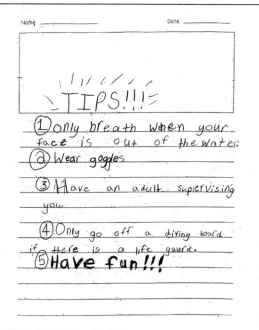

Name ___   Date ___

TIPS!!!

① Only breath when your face is out of the water.

② Wear goggles

③ Have an adult supervising you.

④ Only go off a diving board if there is a life gaurd.

⑤ Have fun!!!

FIG. 13–2   Ebby interests her kindergarten audience by giving tips, using descriptions, and using comparisons about swimming.

Writing Nonfiction Books of All Kinds   BEND III

Writing Nonfiction Books of All Kinds

IN THIS SESSION, you'll teach children that nonfiction writers can mold their information in different ways to write different kinds of nonfiction books.

GETTING READY

✔ Before beginning this session, ask children to look through their own published nonfiction chapter books and choose a favorite to bring to the meeting area for this session.

✔ A bin containing question-and-answer books, how-to books, and stories that teach for you to demonstrate different formats of nonfiction books. A list of recommended books is available on the online resources (see Teaching and Active Engagement) ☜

✔ Your demonstration text from Bend II to show how you reshape the information into different nonfiction formats (see Teaching)

✔ "Nonfiction Writers Can Make . . ." one-day chart, to be revealed one bullet point at a time (see Teaching and Active Engagement) ☜

✔ A nonfiction book in the format of a story that teaches. We use *Growing Frogs* by Vivian French (see Teaching)

W HENEVER WE TEACH WRITING, we are alert for opportunities for transference: that is, we look for ways to raise the level of work to what Norman Webb describes in his research as Depth of Knowledge (DOK) Level 4. At this level, you can look for kids to carry what they've learned into new situations and apply what they've learned with more agency.

Your writers have completed two cycles of the writing process, developing several nonfiction books from start to finish. You've taught them what nonfiction writers do, as well as the moves writers use when they write for an audience. Now, in this third bend, writers will launch into the whole writing cycle again, with a chance to internalize those strategies as well as to transfer them into new contexts.

Your writers will continue to write books for others across this bend, except now they will also consider different *kinds* of books they might write, to write on a familiar topic in a new way. For example, in the last bend, a youngster may have written a book all about dogs for his friend getting a new puppy. Now that same writer might also write a how-to book about dog training. Specifically, writers will choose between writing how-to books, question-and-answer books, or stories that teach.

Across this third bend, writers will take more ownership of their writing and learning lives. You'll invite them to make more choices and they will conduct inquiries into mentor texts with peers and lean on their partnerships to problem solve instead of on you, their teacher.

Today's session asks writers to dive into this new endeavor as best they can. During the minilesson, students will quickly become acquainted with these new kinds of books and select one to try out. Don't get caught up orchestrating the transition from writing all-about books to writing in new forms. An emphasis on independence for your students will simultaneously ask you to have an understanding of their approximations. For today, simply invite writers into this work, leave a few examples of these books on tables as they write, and allow them to give it a go. Above all, have fun with your writers and look for all of the ways they will transfer the work of the unit into their new nonfiction books!

Writing Nonfiction Books of All Kinds

CONNECTION

Set kids up to shape a pretend lump of clay into one or two objects, then ask them to consider how this experience connects to their writing.

"Writers, we're going to start this new bend with some pretending. I need all of you to make a little space on the carpet in front of you, and to look up when you are ready to make believe." I waited, and looked around for kids' eyes to be on me. "You ready? You got a bit of empty space in front of you?" I looked around, checking—knowing that doing so built a drumroll of anticipation.

"Now, will you show me that you have a lump of clay in your hands? This is the clay that professional sculptors use. Feel it in your hands. Move it around, get it nice and pliable."

"Now, sculptors, think for a moment. What will you make with that clay? A rabbit with two ears?" As I talked, I clearly molded my imaginary clay into those two ears. "Or will you make a bird?" I quickly made the "clay" into a bird shape, which I held up. "Get to work and make a super-quick something!"

After a few seconds, I said, "Artists, bring that clay back to a ball, and try making something different. Get to work." I gave the kids just a few seconds to make their next imaginary sculpture, then I invited them to show and explain to each other what they had made. Before they had finished talking, I said, "So why did we do this? You took a ball of clay and shaped it to make one thing, then you reshaped it to make another thing. What does that have to do with the work that writers do?" I again let children talk.

You could, of course, just do this yourself in front of the class instead of involving the kids, and if you make that decision, you could actually hold clay. Alternatively, you could begin by reading page 1 of three books on the same topic, and work your way from there to your teaching point. Do what feels right for your students, but keep this connection brief. Remember, time is of the essence.

The challenge will be to channel your kids to do this in no time at all. Remember your whole minilesson needs to be ten minutes. If time is short, which is likely, you could also just ask the kids to think for a minute about why you asked them to do this. Providing a moment of silence in which you and the kids think about something is far more potent than you may realize.

❖ **Name the teaching point.**

"Today I want to teach you that just as artists can take clay and shape it into one thing and then another, so too, writers can take information about a topic, and shape it into one kind of book, or another, or another."

TEACHING

Remind students that they know how to organize information into all-about books, and begin a chart about the different kinds of nonfiction books that writers can create.

"This means that when a nonfiction writer has expertise about a topic—and you all have that expertise about a lot of topics—the writer can take the information and shape it into one kind of nonfiction book, or another kind of nonfiction book.

"You already know that you can take information about a topic—about bakeries, or race cars, or Spider-Man . . ." I said, citing topics the kids had written about. "And you can shape that information into all-about books with a table of contents and chapters. That's what you did when you wrote the nonfiction chapter books—the ones on your lap today." I uncovered the first bullet point on a new chart.

Nonfiction writers can make . . .

- Nonfiction chapter books

Show how you can shape the information in your demonstration text into a different format: a story that teaches. Emphasize including details that teach into the story.

"Writers, just like you can shape clay in different ways, you can shape your knowledge of your topic in different ways, into different kinds of books. To show you what I mean, let's start and notice different kinds of nonfiction books." I placed a bin containing question-and-answer books, how-to books, and stories that teach on my lap. I began to sift through the bin, building excitement. I pulled out one book.

"Wow, writers, look here." I turned the book *Growing Frogs* toward the class. "This author wrote a story about a little girl and how she learned about frogs. She and her mom go down to the pond and study frogs. It's written like a story, but it teaches all sorts of information about frogs! So cool!"

I placed my bakery book under the document camera. "So, I wonder if I can do that with my book? Let's see if I can reshape this into a story about how I—or maybe a made-up character—learned about bakeries." I paused for a moment to think. "Maybe it could go something like this."

> Natalie and her mom were walking down a New York City street. They saw a sign, "Pete's Bakery." Natalie said, "Let's go in and choose a treat."

I paused for a moment and looked back toward the class. "Okay, now I need to make sure I teach some information about the bakery in this story."

You have options for how you create the chart, "Nonfiction writers can make . . . ," in today's minilesson. You will create the entire chart across the minilesson today with your class; it won't be built up across the bend, so you may choose to write out each bullet point on the chart one by one, or have the bullet points written on slips of paper that you stick onto the chart, or write out the entire chart ahead of time and cover the bullet points with slips of paper that you can remove as you go.

You won't actually write this out in front of your students. Instead, you'll just rehearse it out loud.

When Natalie walked into the bakery, her eyes grew wide. She was shocked to see glass cases with rows of baked treats.

There were large cakes of every flavor. Natalie counted six different types of cakes—chocolate cakes, strawberry shortcakes, carrot cakes, cheesecakes, vanilla cakes, and red velvet cakes.

Natalie also saw loaves of bread. Some were shaped like hot dogs only bigger, and some were shaped like turtles.

Debrief, highlighting the work that you did to shape your information in your bakery book into a new kind of book.

"Writers, did you see what I did there? I took some of the information from my bakery nonfiction chapter book, and I started to shape it into a new kind of book, into a story that teaches." I added "Stories that teach" to the chart.

Notice that this text includes not just one sentence about the cakes in the bakery. There are specific details—numbers, names—about those cakes. The cake information is in one place, the bread in another, too. The information is bucketed.

Nonfiction writers can make . . .

- Nonfiction chapter books
- **Stories that teach**

Channel writers to think about how they might take the information in their book and turn it into a different kind of nonfiction book—a story that teaches.

"Writers, just for a moment, see if you can turn your book into a story that teaches. Close your eyes and think about how it would go in your mind."

As kids thought, I said, "Maybe you will tell the story of someone learning about your topic, whatever it is, like I told about Natalie."

Notice here that there isn't time for students to talk. Moments of silence for thinking are really powerful, and we as teachers don't use them enough.

ACTIVE ENGAGEMENT

Invite partners to study how-to and question-and-answer books, noting what kinds of nonfiction books they are.

"Writers, stories that teach are just one kind of nonfiction book." I tapped the basket of books that now sat at my feet. "Let's find out what other kinds of nonfiction books you can make!

"Quickly, two partnerships meet together. Grab your partner and scooch over next to another partnership close by." As kids organized themselves, I walked around to each group of four and handed them either a how-to book or a question-and-answer book, though they didn't know which kind it was yet.

"Each group has a nonfiction book to explore. Take a moment to look through it with your group and find out what kind of nonfiction book you have."

As kids began to explore texts, I listened in and helped kids name the different kinds of book they were exploring, pointing out key features that would help them rewrite their books into this kind of text.

Convene the class and compile a list of kinds of nonfiction they'd noticed.

After a minute, I called the class back together. "Writers, some of you noticed you were holding how-to books—books that teach the steps for how to do something. Hold those books up high in the air!" Kids holding how-to books held them up for the other groups to see, and I added that kind of book to the chart.

"Some of you were holding a question-and-answer book. Those books teach by asking a question about a topic and then answering it. Hold the question-and-answer books up high!" As kids lifted those up, I added this final kind of nonfiction book to the chart.

Ask students to imagine rewriting your bakery book into one of those kinds of nonfiction. Provide lean coaching to encourage creative thinking.

"Writers, I took my bakery nonfiction chapter book and rewrote it into a story that teaches. Do you think that your group could rewrite my bakery book into a how-to or a question-and-answer book? Get to it!"

As children worked, I coached, "What part of it could be turned into a book that teaches readers to do something?" "What will the steps be? Try teaching each other and have the 'reader' act it out!" "What questions would readers have? What would your answer sound like? Remember to teach all you know!"

LINK

Send students off to try out what they've learned on their own books, offering additional support to students who need more time with mentor texts.

After a few minutes, I reconvened the class. "Writers, take a moment to think about your own book, the one you have in your lap. Think about whether you could rewrite that book as a different kind of nonfiction book—as a story that teaches or a how-to book or maybe a question-and-answer book. Those of you who know which kind of book you are going to make, head off and start writing. Those who need to practice a few more kinds of books before making a decision, stay here on the rug. I'll keep these mentors up front here in this bin in case any of you want to take a peek."

We chose these kinds of books—stories that teach, how-to books, and question-and-answer books—because they allow students to use what they have learned during Bends I and II of this unit. There are other kinds of nonfiction books—ABC books, joke books, and so on—that you could have your students make as well. As you make those decisions, consider the kinds of books you think your students will be able to write fairly independently. For example, question-and-answer books are a bit like the books they have already been writing, but with a slightly different structure. Whatever you decide, remember to make this joyful!

You'll notice that students only practiced one kind of book—either how-to or question-and-answer books. You'll want to keep this brief to give kids a lot of time to actually write these new, fun kinds of nonfiction books. If you feel like your writers need more support with the kind of book they did not yet explore, you might extend the active engagement and have them swap books and orally rehearse the other kind.

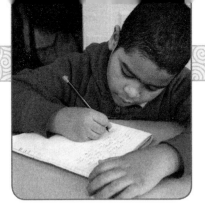

Helping Students Get Off to a Strong Start

THE START OF A NEW BEND is a time to rally your students to give the new work a try. Today, your kids will have four responsibilities. First, they need to settle on a topic, a topic they have already written on, which you prompted them to do at the beginning of today's minilesson. Second, writers need to imagine their topic being written about in one or two different ways and to settle on one way. Then writers will need to plan how they will get started writing about that topic, in that way. Finally they need to draft.

Today's minilesson taught students that they can shape a topic into different sorts of nonfiction writing, and thinking through the different options takes time. Your students may rush ahead and begin rewriting without taking time to explore the ways their books could be molded. You might show some of those writers—the more advanced—how to imagine various possibilities for revision, delaying closure. Generally, the more experienced a writer is, the more he or she revises during rehearsal and drafting, not during revision. You might tell writers that the children's author Robert Munsch story-tells anything he writes *one hundred times* before drafting it, and suggest that your students would profit from yet more rehearsal. Rehearsal can become a time for revision, in the largest sense of the word.

Once students have decided to write a particular kind of book, you will want to suggest that they read and reread a mentor text or two that represents their new image, this time studying the mentor texts closely, thinking about all the decisions that the author had to make. Encourage writers to notice not only what the author did—that is, what is contained in the book—but also to notice *how* the author did it. What can they notice about this table of contents? How is this like a story even though it teaches?

One more thing that a writer needs to do before launching into the writing is to gather the paper he or she needs to construct a new book. Most writers will use their rehearsal or plan to determine the number of pages needed, while others will grab a booklet or stack of single pages and start writing. If some writers seem stymied,

you could offer up a quick tip: "Writers think about the big parts of their book—the number of questions, or big events of their story or the number of steps—to determine how many pages they need for their book. They also know they can add or take away pages as they get working!"

Your job today is to help writers get started and to offer quick tips and coaching to keep them moving from idea to rehearsal to drafting!

MID-WORKSHOP TEACHING
Using Other Writers as a Resource

"Writers, can you look up here for a moment? Raise your hand if you are writing a question-and-answer book. Tap your nose if you are writing narrative nonfiction. Stand up if you are writing a how-to book."

When all of the kids were gesturing I continued, "How cool! We all have different plans and are writing different kinds of nonfiction books! Whenever I'm trying something new, it helps to see lots of examples of that kind of work. Right now, could you look around for someone who is writing the same kind of book as you? Look for the same signal!

"In a moment, could you meet with that person and switch books? When you switch, study the kinds of things that writer is doing. Use that time to get some ideas for what you could do in your book, too."

I signaled for writers to meet up to learn about their new kinds of books from each other. Then after a few minutes I signaled for everyone to return to his or her own writing.

Writing with an Audience in Mind

Remind writers they are writing for an audience. Coach one writer as she selects an audience and writes a reminder Post-it, then ask all writers to do the same.

"Writers, can you bring your folders with your new writing and Post-its inside, and gather on the rug?" The class quickly came over, materials in hand, and I continued. "Now that you are trying out these new kinds of books," I pointed to the "Nonfiction writers can make . . ." chart, "that doesn't mean you should forget all about writing for others. In your excitement to get started on your new books today, you forgot something *super* important. You forgot to pick an audience!" I feigned shock and the class followed suit.

I picked up a mentor text and opened to the inside. "I bet you've seen the messages inside the cover of books before—the dedication." The class nodded. "Well, one thing a dedication can do is let readers know who the book is for. Writing a dedication might be a good audience reminder for your new books. You already know how to pick an audience, so that part will be easy! Could you also now think about *why* you chose to write your audience that kind of book?" Writers nodded their heads.

"Marilyn, can you bring your new book up here?" Marilyn came up with her question-and-answer swimming book. "Marilyn, who is your audience? Who will you dedicate this book about swimming to?" She thought for a moment and responded, "Little kids."

I responded, "I'm wondering why you chose to write a question-and-answer book." Marilyn paused to think, and Jake jumped in, "Maybe because little kids ask a million questions all the time!" Marilyn smiled and nodded, "They need a lot of answers. They have a lot to learn!"

"Writers," I turned back to the rest of the class, "it's your turn to think, who is your audience and why are you writing *this* kind of book for that audience? Write it on a Post-it and stick it on the inside cover of your book as a dedication. You can look back at the Post-it to keep your audience in mind."

It is likely that students spent more time considering the kind of book to make than considering audience during today's minilesson, so now is a perfect time for them to reflect on who they are writing for. Audience continues to be important as writers will not only need to consider what readers will want to know but how they can best teach them—through a question-and-answer book, a how-to, or a story that teaches.

Leaning on Authors as Mentors

O NE WAY THAT THE UNITS OF STUDY IN OPINION, INFORMATION, and Narrative Writing help students build toward independence is by teaching them how to learn from other texts. Look across any unit, in any grade, and you are bound to find a handful of sessions that invite writers to study the ways in which published authors work.

If you taught the first second-grade unit, *Lessons from the Masters*, then your writers spent a good deal of time getting to know Jane Yolen and her narrative craft by studying *Owl Moon*. The first bend of this unit built on that background. You invited your young writers to study nonfiction texts noticing, as best they could, the ways in which *nonfiction* authors teach their readers.

Today's minilesson offers writers another opportunity to study ways in which nonfiction writers craft different kinds of nonfiction texts. You'll group students together so that those working on the same kind of writing are sitting and working alongside each other. The idea, as always, is that writers will study mentor texts as best they can. Of course you will find opportunities to chime in and guide kids along the way and help them name out particular moves.

You and your colleagues who are also teaching this unit may find it helpful to gather together before the lesson and study the kinds of texts you are offering students. You can develop your own lists of writing moves—much like your youngsters will do today. In this way you will be ready to support kids as they uncover the ways in which authors teach how to make something or teach through a story.

You will also find it helpful to leave a bit of extra time at the end of your workshop today for a gallery walk. In today's share you'll invite writers to learn from one another by displaying their books and inquiry charts as resources for others to use as they prepare to write new kinds of texts tomorrow. Although it may seem early in the bend for writers to start another book, you will want to remind them, and yourself, that they can always go back to books that are unfinished as the bend continues. Repeated practice continues to be important for your writers.

IN THIS SESSION, you'll teach children that nonfiction writers use books as writing resources. They study different kinds of books and think "How can I use craft moves like these in my own books?"

GETTING READY

- ✔ Large Post-it notes labelled with the different kinds of nonfiction books and placed around the rug (see Connection)

- ✔ Ask students to bring the nonfiction book they started writing yesterday with them to the rug (see Connection)

- ✔ Post-its and a variety of nonfiction mentor texts of different kinds to distribute to groups (see Teaching and Active Engagement)

- ✔ A sheet of chart paper and a marker for each group (see Link)

Leaning on Authors as Mentors

CONNECTION

◆ COACHING

Acknowledge that starting something new, like writing new kinds of books, can leave a lot of unanswered questions.

"Writers, as you head over to the rug today with your new nonfiction books that you started on yesterday, please note that you'll be sitting somewhere new! Find the Post-it with the kind of book you are writing written on it and sit with other students who are writing the same kind of book.

"Yesterday you started writing brand-new nonfiction books. Not only that—you were writing new *kinds* of nonfiction books, kinds of nonfiction books you probably had never written before. Do you know what I noticed? Because these kinds of books are brand-new to you, you had so many questions! It seemed like every time I looked up, a few of you had a question. Did you notice that, too?" Kids nodded in agreement.

"Well, here's the thing. It's *totally normal*. When you want to make something that you haven't made before, you usually have lots of questions. But the key thing is that you need to learn to answer those questions by yourself." I paused for dramatic effect. "It's true! Today I'll teach you how."

❧ **Name a question that will guide the inquiry.**

"Today I want to teach you that when writers want to write a kind of text they have never written before, they don't have to do that work alone. You can *always* find yourself a mentor. Just find books that are like those you want to write, and let the authors of those books mentor you."

TEACHING AND ACTIVE ENGAGEMENT

Remind students about how an inquiry works, then distribute mentor texts and Post-its to each group of writers.

"You might remember during our last unit, when you were writing small moment stories, you investigated *Owl Moon*. You found powerful parts and thought, 'How did Jane Yolen write like this?' Writers, since you've already done this kind of inquiry work with me, I thought that you would be ready to try it out on your own!"

Today's connection highlights the contrast between dependence and independence. To foster independence in your writers, it's important that you help them learn how to problem solve and use resources other than yourself, both of which you will do throughout today's session.

If you did not teach Lessons from the Masters *and inquiry is new to your class, you might choose to lead them through an inquiry together before letting kids meet in groups to take on inquiry of these texts by themselves.*

I distributed mentor texts to each group according to the kind of book they were writing. "Writers, you now have a mentor text or two that matches the kind of book you are writing near you on the rug. In a moment, you and your group will read that mentor text together, noticing parts that draw you in and thinking, 'What did the author do here that I could try in my writing?' Then, as you find special ways that the kind of book you're making teaches, you might stick a Post-it on that spot and record it, just like we did when we studied *Owl Moon*."

Circulate the room, listening to the ways that students are analyzing their mentor texts. Provide lean coaching to help develop their thinking.

I coached the group working on how-to books. "What are you noticing?" I asked.

"Well, there are steps," Amanda offered.

"Yes, I bet the how-to books you've written have steps, too. What did this author do that you haven't done yet and could try?"

"Well, there are action words. And look," Morgan called, pointing to the picture. "The same action is in the picture, too!"

"Oh, so there are specific actions in the words *and* the pictures?" I asked. The group nodded and began jotting that strategy on a Post-it as I quickly moved toward the next group.

I then circulated to the other groups, and coached by saying things like, "What are you noticing?" "What could you try in your own writing? "Is there something special that this author did that you're going to try?"

LINK

Direct groups to remove the Post-its from inside mentor texts, with their collected craft moves, and stick them onto chart paper, creating a resource.

"Writers, I hate to pry you away from your investigation, but I want you to have plenty of time to head off and use the craft moves you found to revise your books so that they teach even more!"

I quickly gave each group of students a piece of chart paper and a marker. "Choose someone in your group to write the name of your group at the top of your chart paper. Your group's name is the kind of book you'll be writing, so the Stories that Teach group will write 'Stories that Teach' at the top of their chart paper. Then, gather up the Post-its from inside your books and stick them on the chart paper." I gave kids just a moment to do this.

If you know from yesterday's work that one kind of book or another is very popular in your class, plan to have more than one mentor text for that kind of book handy during this part of the minilesson. Invite any larger groups to break off into smaller groups of four kids before you distribute books. Making each group a bit smaller will allow all writers to remain engaged during the minilesson.

Having a few key strategies for each kind of book in your back pocket will be important for your coaching during this part of the minilesson.

Try to avoid getting caught up with any one group for more than a minute or so. It will be tempting to coach each group extensively in an effort to get kids off to a good start. Instead, trust in their abilities to notice and name author's moves as best they can and move on.

Channel students to use the chart they made to plan their writing work for today, then send them off to write.

"Quickly, look at your chart, the strategies you've collected, and make a plan for what you will try today to make your book teach as much as it can." After a half of a minute I continued. "It seems like you all now have a plan! Let's find some space for you to each hang your charts. You might choose to write right in front of the chart so you can remember all of the different ways that your kind of book should teach readers.

"Before we set up each group with some space in our classroom, I want to remind you that you know how to answer your own questions. I bet that you'll end up having more questions today, but the exciting news is that you can now answer those questions on your own! You can pick up a mentor text and use it to think, 'How does this book teach?'"

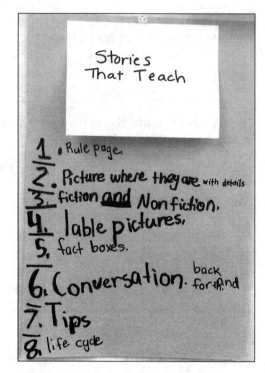

FIG. 15–1   Chart of strategies learned from a mentor text for stories that teach

Focusing on the Work at Hand

AS YOU CONFER WITH GROUPS and individual writers today, it will be important for you to keep an eye on what matters most. For example, it matters that children study the work of other authors and notice the ways in which these authors teach information. It also matters that your kids come up with their own observations about what the author has done and why. You can't expect that your youngsters will have the same kinds of observations and insights that you, as an adult, would have. Allow them to be second-graders, and acknowledge their approximations as they create their own charts and use them to craft their books.

If you find that a group needs a bit of a nudge to notice and name a few more writing moves, you might offer your support by studying a page or two alongside them. Ask writers to point to parts of the page that stand out. Then work together to name a move or two in a way that kids will understand and remember how to use it. Remind writers to consider how or why they think the author chose to use one move or another. This will help them think about how to transfer the work into their own books.

Then, too, it matters that writers look at their own books and think not only about what they will write, but also *how* they will write it. Perhaps you pull up to a writer who looks overwhelmed by all of the choices she has for crafting her stories-that-teach book. She may benefit from some support to determine just two or three techniques to use. You might start your conference with a nod toward her group's chart, "I see your group noticed a lot of cool things about stories that teach! I bet you want to try all of these moves, right?" The writer will surely nod along. "Sometimes, when there are so many new things to try, it can be overwhelming. I find it helpful to pick just a few moves to try at first, just to get the hang of it. Then I try those moves across all my pages as a way to practice. Should we try that?" You could then invite the writer to reread her group's chart and select a few moves she's excited to try all across her book. Maybe she decides to add little facts to each of her pages and to include some zoom-in pictures. Stay long enough for her to get started, and then remind her that she can look back at the chart any time to pick her next writing move by herself. You can always check in on her later and give an encouraging word.

While writing different kinds of nonfiction books gives your youngsters lots to explore—new kinds of books and writing moves—it will be important for you to remember during your conferences to think of one step forward a child might make, and to teach just that. Resist the urge to teach one thing after another in an effort to make their first attempts into masterpieces.

MID-WORKSHOP TEACHING
Problem Solving with Your Group

"Writers, let me interrupt you, just for a moment. I just had to share how different today looks! Instead of looking out across the classroom and seeing hands waving me over with questions, I see writers who are using mentor texts to answer questions on their own! Give yourselves a quick pat on the back!

"Before you turn back to your books, I wanted to give you one more tip—another way that you can solve problems. When you have a question, you can ask a mentor text, but you can *also* ask your group.

"Just a moment ago, Sara, over in the how-to book group, couldn't figure out how to write her next step. I overheard her ask her group for help, and you know what? They came up with lots of solutions for her! One group member said, 'Just act it out!' Another group member said, 'Use the words *next* or *then*.' Those few suggestions helped answer Sara's question. So, writers, don't hesitate to get help from the group members sitting around you if you need it!"

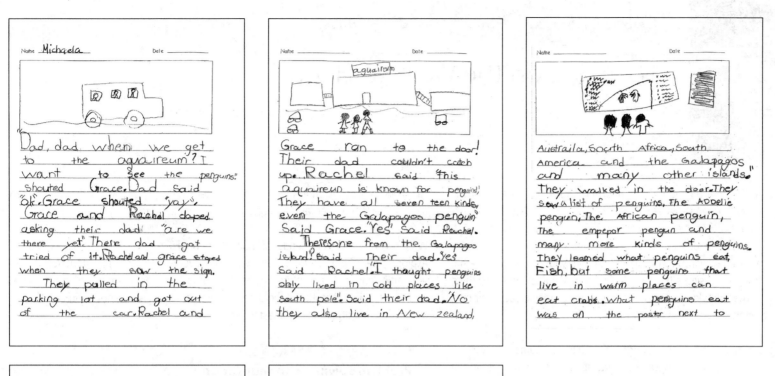

"Dad, dad when we get to the aquaireum? I want to see the penguins!" shouted Grace. Dad said "Ok". Grace shouted "yay". Grace and Rachel doped asking their dad "are we there yet". There dad got tried of it. Rachel and grace stoped when they saw the sign. They pulled in the parking lot and got out of the car. Rachel and

Grace ran to the door! Their dad couldn't catch up. Rachel said "This aquaireun is known for penguins." They have all seven teen kinds, even the Galapagos penguin" Said Grace. "Yes" Said Rachel. Theresone from the Galapagos island" Said Their dad. "Yes" Said Rachel. "I thought penguins obly lived in cold places like south pole". Said their dad. "No they also live in New zealand,

Austraila, South Africa, South America and the Galapagos and many other islands." They walked in the door. They saw a list of penguins. The ADDelie penguin, The African penguin, The empepor pengun and many more kinds of penguins. They learned what penguins eat, Fish, but some penguins that live in warm places can eat crabs. What penguins eat was on the poster next to

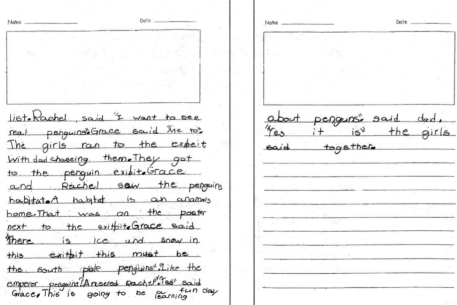

list. Rachel said "I want to see real penguins". Grace said "Me to". The girls ran to the exibeit with dad chaseing them. They got to the penguin exibit. Grace and Rachel saw the penguins habitat. A habitat is an anamals home. That was on the poster next to the exitbit. Grace said "There is ice and snow in this exitbit this must be the south pole penguins". "Like the emperor penguins? Answered Rachel. "Yes" said Grace, This is going to be a fun day learning

about penguins" said dad. "Yes it is" the girls said together.

FIG. 15–2 Michaela uses a strategy she learned from her mentor text for stories that teach. She teaches information through her character's conversations.

Gaining Inspiration from Mentor Texts and Peers' Writing

Invite students to take a gallery walk of each other's writing to determine what kind of book they want to make next.

"Writers, can you look up here for a moment? I won't ask you to gather on the rug today, at least not right away. You've been working for the last two days to take your expert topic and shape it into something new—a new kind of book. I bet you're itching to get started on *another* kind of nonfiction book.

"One way to choose your next kind of book might be to go on a gallery walk. When people go into a gallery they look all around at the artwork or exhibit noticing the pieces they like. On a writing gallery walk, you can look at the mentor texts, each other's books, and the charts that groups made for their kind of book. As you walk you can think, 'What kind of book do I want to make next?'" The class was game.

"Take just a minute to set up your display with your books and your group chart." I helped groups organize and after a minute, the gallery walk commenced. I instructed groups to walk to the left and stop in front of the next group's display. "Okay, writers, take one minute and explore the kind of book you're standing in front of! Remember to think, 'What kind of book will I make next?'" Kids began to flip through each other's books and read the group charts. After about a minute or so kids rotated to the left and continued on that way until everyone had been to each display.

"As you wrap up looking at the display for the last kind of writing, quickly head on over to the rug." The class gathered. "Do you all have a plan? Thumbs up if you know how you will shape your information next." A sea of thumbs appeared in front of me. "How exciting! Almost everyone has a new plan. Turn to your partner and tell them the kind of book you'll be starting."

Today's share continues the independent spirit of this bend. The gallery walk invites writers to glean what they find important and helpful from other writer's work. They can then use this new learning to inform their choice for a final book of the unit.

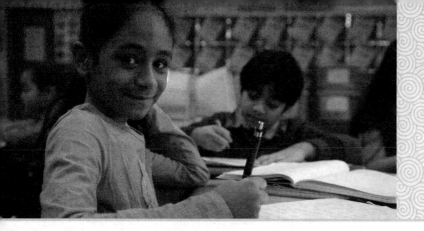

Writers Use Reminders to Craft New Books

IN THIS SESSION, you'll teach children that writers use all that they know about writing nonfiction whenever they write.

GETTING READY

✔ A blank booklet to model how you plan out your writing (see Connection)

✔ "To Teach an Audience" anchor chart (see Teaching, Active Engagement, and Share) ✋

✔ "Partner Work" one-day chart (see Share) ✋

ACROSS BEND II, students learned how to write for an audience by each day adding to their repertoire of writing moves. One day they learned how to help their readers picture information while the next day they learned to hook a reader's interest from the start. Continuing the previous session's push for independence, today you'll suggest that children need not wait for another bit of teaching, instead they can lean on all that they learned across the previous bend to work in ways that make sense for their new books. You'll explain to them that now that they know so much about writing nonfiction books, it is up to them to decide what will make their books better right from the start.

If writers are writing new books today, which will hopefully be the case for most students, you will encourage them to use the anchor chart from Bend II as they rehearse and draft another kind of book, perhaps about the same topic.

"Children can lean on all that they learned to work in ways that make sense for their new book."

Of course, your hope will be that your students will remember the mentor text lesson you just taught them and will study exemplars of the kind of writing they plan to make as they get started on this new writing project. In the conferring and small-group work section, we remind you that writers can turn to other resources, such as mentor texts, to add to their repertoire of moves, and that much of what writers notice in these texts will support them as they continue to write for others—teaching information and capturing interest.

As the unit nears to a close, you'll want children to begin to take more ownership of their own writing decisions and craft moves. After all, in just a few days they will be ready to share their books with audiences of all kinds.

Writers Use Reminders to Craft New Books

CONNECTION

Demonstrate how you take your topic and rehearse a new kind of book as a way to get started. Invite writers to quickly do the same with their own topic and new kind of book.

"Writers, I know you made plans to start a new kind of book today. Before we do anything else, will you remember the book you are planning to write? How many of you will be writing a how-to book?" I signaled for those youngsters to show their intent with a thumbs up, and then I asked, "How many of you think you will be asking a new question on the top of each page, and then answering the question underneath?" Again, those children signaled.

"Let's take a moment to plan how you can take your old book and rewrite it as a different kind of book," I said. "I might rewrite my bakery book as a how-to," and I picked up a booklet and started touching the pages, talking out loud about how the book would go if I did that. "It might go like this."

How to Learn about Bakeries

"Hmm, . . . What was the first step to learning about bakeries? Oh! I know, going into one. So my book might start:

How to Learn about Bakeries
Step 1: Walk down the street and see a bakery.
Step 2: Push the door open, smell the good smells.

"If I were writing a question-and-answer book, would I write in steps?" The kids chimed, "No," and I nodded. "I'd need to think of questions like, 'How can you learn about bakeries?' And 'What do bakeries sell?'

"Right now, will each of you think how your book will go?" I left some silence for the kids to do that thinking. After a bit I said, "Pick up an imaginary blank booklet," and I did the same. "Touch the first page and silently, in your mind, whisper what you will write—the exact words—on page 1, then page 2."

This part of the minilesson is important and sets writers up for today's teaching. Because writers will only have an idea of the kind of book they are making, from today's gallery walk, they will need a moment to consider how that book might go right now during the connection.

Notice that you only orally rehearse this version of your book—writing-it-in-the-air with your voice. Later on, you will revise this initial version again in the air.

I did this same work in front of the class, silently.

"Now, writers, after you have planned how your book will go, it will be time to write your new books. But, writers, I have one *huge* tip to give you."

❖ **Name the teaching point.**

"Today I want to teach you that learning to write well involves trying new things, but it also involves remembering to do everything you learned earlier. Sometimes it helps to have ways to remind yourself of the things you already know to do."

TEACHING

Tell students that it helps people to keep lists on hand that are reminders of things a person has already learned to do, and to use those lists as to-do lists.

"Before you actually get started writing this next kind of book, it will be important to think of all you've learned about writing. You know so many things about writing, but here's the thing: it is easy to forget the things you know. One way that I keep from forgetting things is that I write lists, and I use lists to remind me of things I want to do.

"If I want to remember to bring a bunch of stuff to school for our writing workshop, I jot down a list of what I can't forget. The good news for you as writers is the list already exists. You don't have to make your own list of all the things you can't forget about writing nonfiction. You just have to remember to reach for the list, to use the list. Let's do that now."

Review the first two bullets of the anchor chart from Bend II with writers.

I unfastened the "To Teach an Audience . . ." anchor chart from its place on the wall and placed it on the easel, front and center. "Let's read the start of this chart together. As you read, will you think about what each Post-it is really telling you to do? Each of these Post-its is meant to remind you of a whole lot of work that you have learned to do." I pointed to the title and signaled for the class to join in a shared reading of it and of the first two Post-its.

Inviting students to activate their thinking around their new book sets them up to later move into the work of revising how they will teach about their topic. Writers need to be able to move from an initial rehearsal of their book into a more revised version so that they write in more sophisticated ways right from the start.

Grant Wiggins's research on transfer reminds us that students will not cue themselves to use prior knowledge in new situations unless we remind them to do this. You can help students transfer what they've learned to new contexts by naming the opportunity for the transfer of knowledge explicitly. You make transfer easier and more likely by using the same language and visuals.

To Teach an Audience

- Think, "Who is my audience?" and "What will they want to learn?"
- Help readers picture the information.
  - Add description.
  - Add comparisons.
- Hook readers with an interesting lead.
  - Ask a question.
  - Introduce the chapter's topic with pop-out words.
- Clear up confusion.
  - Answer the readers' questions.
  - Fix spelling and punctuation mistakes.
- Set goals and meet them page after page.

"Whew, that is a lot to think about! I've got to think about who my readers are for my *How to Learn about Bakeries* book—and you have to think who *your* readers are for your books, too. Hmm, . . .

"What are you thinking for your book?" I gave students a brief moment to think.

Demonstrate using the anchor chart as a reminder to write for an audience. Revise your earlier rehearsal of your new book.

"Before, my other bakery book was for the teachers at my school who love treats, but I think they know about bakeries. What I am thinking is that my mom lives way far away, and she has never visited a New York City bakery. So now I think I am writing for my mom. That gives me an idea for how I might change around the start of this book. Instead of starting like this," I said, as I spoke my thoughts aloud.

How to Learn about Bakeries

Step 1: Walk down the street and see a bakery.
Step 2: Push the door open, smell the good smells.

"I think I will call it *How to Learn about NYC Bakeries*. And maybe I will say, 'When you visit New York City, you will want to visit the bakeries.' Then I can get into the steps. Does that make sense?

"Writers, do you see how I'm using the chart to remind me of things we have studied that are important for me to remember to do?"

Most seven-year-old writers do not revise their plans. Instead they make a plan and get right to the work of drafting. Your demonstration of revising right from the start is important. You convey that revision isn't something one waits for at the end of the process, rather it is something that writers do constantly, throughout their work on a piece.

ACTIVE ENGAGEMENT

Set partners up to orally rehearse their books, drawing on all that they know and using the anchor chart to coach each other.

"Writers, are you feeling ready to give it a try? Think back to your plan for how your book will go," I said and left a second for them to remember their plan. "Now, keep in mind that you have a list of things to remember," and I pointed to the list and reread the first two bullets. "Partner 1, share your plan with your Partner 2 and then, out loud, rehearse what you will write when you are writing for the particular audience you have in mind. Get to it, partners!"

As partners began planning their next books, orally rehearsing what they would write, I acted as a ghost partner, whispering to Partner 2s with ways they could prompt Partner 1s. I whispered prompts like, "Who is the audience?" and "What will your audience want to learn?"

LINK

Send students off to write their books, using charts as needed to remind them of their prior learning.

After partners had a few minutes to rehearse, I called them back together. "Writers, it seems like you all have exciting work ahead of you! The important thing to keep in mind is that you can use all that you've learned, all that you know, as you write new kinds of books. Look around the room at the charts if you need reminders of that learning so that you can bring it forward into your books."

When coaching partnerships it is important to think about your role. Sometimes you play the role of a proficient partner—overtly modeling the behaviors or conversation you wish your writers to emulate. Other times your role is less front and center. As a "ghost" partner you position yourself behind the coaching partner, in this case Partner 2, and whisper helpful prompts. In this way you don't insert yourself into the middle of the partnership but instead remain behind the scenes.

Because only Partner 1 was able to rehearse in the active engagement today you might decide to invite all Partner 2s to stay at the rug for a moment. They can partner up to rehearse their new books quickly. This will allow all writers to begin their new books with a solid plan in mind.

Using Resources to Spark New Teaching

TODAY DURING THE MINILESSON, you helped students recall what they know about writing for an audience, and you reminded them to keep their audience in mind as they write. You mentioned a bit about the work of doing that, but there is a lot more you can teach today during your one-to-one conferences and small groups.

The unit is nearing an end, so for your more experienced writers, you'll be able to support them in tackling work that is a bit of a stretch. Perhaps you'll teach them that they can improve their writing by rereading it as if they are the reader, the intended audience. Pretending to be a stranger to the text, they can try to notice places where they'll be confused and generate the questions that readers are likely to ask. Then, they can go back to their pages and add flaps or half-page inserts on which they answer those questions.

You can also teach your students that if they want readers to love, love, love their books, they might try adding those things that you think your young writers are ready to try. Perhaps you'll tell students that readers love anecdotes, or stories—as indeed they do. Children could think about how to insert stories into their books, using phrases such as "One time, I . . ." or "I once heard the story about a time when . . ." Of course, readers also adore details. Your bakery book is better because you named the kinds of cakes in the bakery's display case and told about bread shaped like a turtle. Have your students worked as hard as they can to add precise details? Your anchor chart from Bend II states that writing for readers also can mean adding comparisons or descriptions, and of course helping students with that work will be no easy task. Be sure you remind them that whenever a writer wants to do something, it can help to find a mentor text and to study what the author has done.

Perhaps a few of your writers could benefit from digging deeper into a mentor text to notice more specifically how or why an author uses one move or another and then work to transfer that move into their books. Many of the things that writers notice in their mentor texts are ways to add more specific information or capture an audience's interest—work you reminded writers of in today's minilesson. For example, writers composing stories that teach will have to think about the ways they are delivering the information the reader may want to know. A closer look at a mentor text will reveal that this could be in the form of dialogue between characters, or bit-by-bit action, or even facts that teach housed in separate sections of the pages. If a writer were looking for places to teach more information in her own book, you could pull a mentor text such as *Growing Frogs* close with that writer and notice how the author uses facts that teach on many of the pages. As you look, thinking about how the author does this and why, you could help the writer start to notice when that author adds important facts—such as underneath a big event in the story, or when the reader will need more specific information to understand what is happening in the story. You could then invite the writer to look for similar places in her story and mark them with Post-its as a signal to herself that those would be important places to add in facts that teach.

(continues)

MID-WORKSHOP TEACHING
Becoming the Reader of Your Own Writing

"Writers, can I have your attention up here?" I asked and waited until I had everyone's eyes. "One way to write for readers is to actually try out being the reader of your writing. I know you aren't done writing this new book yet, but will you pause for a minute and shift from being a writer to being a reader?

"You'll reread your piece—but here is the trick. Reread it to yourself, in a whispery voice that only you can hear. And as you read, notice the places where you can make your writing *even* better. Listen for the places where you can add more information or use descriptions or comparisons to make information more interesting. Are you ready? Get started!"

For writers whose main goal is more writing today, you may help them focus on strategies that produce a lot of writing. In how-to books, this might include adding in tips and warnings or explaining how or why after teaching a step. You may want to remind writers that they not only want to add more to their books, but they also want to make sure their writing is appealing to their readers. Strong action words, zoom-in pictures, a list, keywords, or pop-out words will not add much volume to a student's writing, but they are helpful and create interest for the reader.

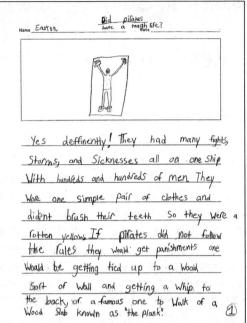

Name Easton   Did pirates have a tough life?

Yes deffinently! They had many fights, storms, and sicknesses all on one ship with hundreds and hundreds of men. They wore one simple pair of clothes and didin't brush their teeth so they were a rotten yellow. If pirates did not follow the rules they would get punishments one would be getting tied up to a wood sort of wall and getting a whip to the back, or a famous one to walk of a wood slab known as "the plank".

①

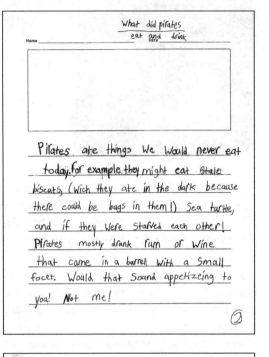

Name ____   What did pirates eat and drink

Pirates ate things we would never eat today. For example they might eat stale biscuts, (wich they ate in the dark because there could be bugs in them!) Sea turtle, and if they were starved each other! Pirates mostly drank rum or wine that came in a barrel with a small focet. Would that sound appetizeing to you! Not me!

②

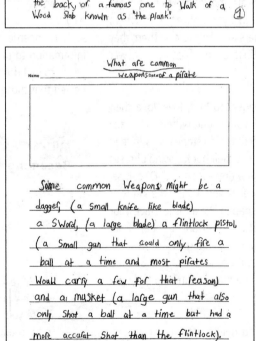

Name ____   What are common weapons of a pirate

Some common weapons might be a dagger, (a small knife like blade) a sword, (a large blade) a flintlock pistol, (a small gun that could only fire a ball at a time and most pirates would carry a few for that reason) and a musket (a large gun that also only shot a ball at a time but had a more accurat shot than the flintlock).

③

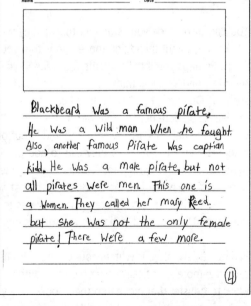

Name ____   What are some famous pirates?

Blackbeard was a famous pirate. He was a wild man when he fought. Also, another famous pirate was captian kidd. He was a male pirate, but not all pirates were men. This one is a women. They called her mary Reed. but she was not the only female pirate! There were a few more.

④

FIG. 16–1 Easton uses examples and embeds definitions across his questions-and-answer book about pirates as a way to add more specific information for his readers.

Leaning on Partners for Writing Support

Remind students of their earlier partner work. Encourage partners to choose how they will support each other.

I stood in the middle of the room and called for attention. "Writers, today I won't gather you at the meeting area. Instead could you take your writing and meet with your partner? Find a spot to sit together—make sure you're not too close to another partnership."

As writers moved toward their partners and settled into a spot I continued, "Today you used the chart 'To Teach an Audience' in new ways—as you crafted your new kinds of books. Thumbs up if you found that chart helpful." A sea of thumbs rose up into the air.

"I'm wondering if some of your partner work from Bend II would be helpful as well?" Kids nodded eagerly. "Here's a little menu of all the ways you've worked with your partner." I revealed a chart that listed the ways that partners worked together.

"Take a moment with your partner to look over the menu and think about the kind of partner work that will be most helpful for you today. Do you need your partner to give you feedback or write a review? Or maybe you just need your partner to listen as you rehearse your book? Make a choice and start working together!"

Partners Lend a Hand
Offering Feedback from One Nonfiction Writer to Another

IN THIS SESSION, you'll teach children that writing partners can help improve each other's writing by giving each other feedback.

GETTING READY

✔ Before this session, prepare a partnership to give a fishbowl demonstration of providing constructive feedback (see Teaching).

✔ "Partners Give Useful Feedback" one-day chart (see Teaching)

✔ Students will need their writing folders, with their own writing and a copy of the Information Writing Checklist (see Active Engagement and Mid-Workshop Teaching).

✔ Small white boards and dry erase markers for students to practice spelling (see Conferring and Small-Group Work)

✔ Extra copies of the Information Writing Checklist, grades 1 and 2, for students to cut into flaps and use for setting goals (see Conferring and Small-Group Work)

AT THE BEGINNING OF THIS UNIT, you rallied writers to become like the nonfiction authors in their classroom library, authors such as Seymour Simon and Gail Gibbons. To become like these writers, you taught children to write about their topics of expertise and to write in ways that captivate an audience. You also taught children to live the lives of a nonfiction author—to gather topics across all parts of their day, to set writing goals, and to apprentice themselves to the kinds of books they wish to make.

Today you will remind writers of one more way they can become like the nonfiction authors you introduced them to—they can call on a community of other writers for support. Many professional writers have a community of writer friends to whom they turn for feedback and suggestions, both when they are developing an idea and later when they are revising. They bounce ideas off one another, pose questions, and reflect on what is and isn't yet working, checking to be sure their writing has the intended effect. Today you will teach your writers how to call on their partners for precise and supportive feedback. You will show them how to communicate around a shared set of criteria—the Information Writing Checklist—and to be clear about when a writer is and is not meeting his or her intended goal or goals.

"Writers have a community of friends to whom they turn for feedback and suggestions."

As writers receive feedback and set off to write and revise with great intent, you may decide to use your conferring and small-group time to gather groups of writers who have similar goals and invite them to extend their support to one another as they work. Later in the share, writers will take a bit of time on their own to determine the books they wish to prepare for the final celebration.

Partners Lend a Hand

Offering Feedback from One Nonfiction Writer to Another

CONNECTION

◆ COACHING

Rally students to work together to help provide each other with feedback, reminding them of the upcoming writing celebration.

"You will never guess what happened to me yesterday." I paused to create some drama. "As you know, I've been writing so much about bakeries. It made me hungry for a freshly baked treat! After school, I walked into a bakery and bought a cookie, and as I was about to leave, the cashier asked, 'Would you mind leaving us some feedback?' He handed me a feedback card. It had a space for me to write something I liked about the bakery and a space for me to leave the bakery something to get better at.

"You're getting close to the end of the unit, to your big celebration, where you'll share your published books with one another and add them to the classroom library. The thing is, you still have some work to do. There is no way that I can make it around our classroom to meet with each of you today. Do you think you could help each other the way I helped the bakery?"

"Yes!" the class called in unison.

❖ **Name the teaching point.**

"Today I want to teach you that writing partners can give each other feedback to help them set and meet goals. One way you can do this is by using the checklist to guide you. You can look to see what your partner is doing well and what he or she may need to practice."

TEACHING

Organize a writing partnership in a fishbowl as a demonstration for giving effective feedback. Invite the rest of the class to observe and note their behaviors.

"Writers, would you please gather around and make a half circle here in the meeting area? Be sure to stay next to your partner." The class quickly organized themselves into a half circle, leaving the front area on the rug open.

It's helpful for the class to know when the end of a writing unit is approaching. Many teachers even post end-of-unit celebrations on the calendar so that kids can be working with a date in mind, ensuring that their books are ready for publication.

When the class was organized, I said, "You have just created a fishbowl, which means you sit on the outside watching what is happening on the inside, just like you would watch a fish in a bowl. In a moment, I'll invite a partnership to come into the center to practice giving feedback. You'll sit and watch as they meet, but you'll also have a big job to do! As you're watching, you'll be thinking about how they work together to give useful feedback. You can think, 'What are they saying?' and 'What are they doing?'"

I continued, "Lily and Jay, would you come to the center? Bring your folder and your checklist."

Lily and Jay sat down in the center of the fishbowl, sitting side by side. Jay pulled out a copy of the Information Writing Checklist. Lily followed suit, smoothing out her checklist and taking one of her books out of her folder.

Jay turned to Lily and said, "I can help you with your writing first." She agreed.

Jay placed his copy of the checklist in between them. "Let's read the checklist. What do you want me to help you check in your book?" he asked. Lily pointed to the elaboration section of the checklist that read, "I used different kinds of information in my writing." Together the writers looked back and forth between the checklist and Lily's writing.

Jay said, "I like how you have a lot of facts on every page. I think you could practice adding tips or definitions. Like here," Jay pointed toward Lily's writing. "You could give a definition and say what the word *tusk* means."

Lily nodded and leaned over to revise her writing. Then she said, "Could you help me find another place?"

"Freeze!" I stopped Lily and Jay and turned back toward the rest of the class. "Writers, those partners really worked together! Jay didn't just say, 'Your writing is great' and move on to his own. No way! Think about what they did to help make Lily's writing better, and turn and tell your partner."

Listen as partnerships debrief. Gather the class back together and chart the behaviors that children noticed, naming them as transferable partnership behaviors.

I moved around the circle, listening in and helping children name the behaviors they saw. Then I gathered students back together to recap what we saw. "Writers, I heard so many of you talking about what you saw this partnership do that you could try. Let's try to make a list." I revealed the "Partners Give Useful Feeback" chart and said, "I heard some of you mention that both partners were sitting together with their materials, checklists, and writing, in between them." I touched the second heading. "Partners were using the checklist. They named compliments and something to practice." I pointed to the third heading and continued, "They practiced the new goal together."

During this minilesson, students study the behaviors and language of a partnership that effectively gives feedback. The class acts as researchers, studying the partnership to transfer productive behaviors to their own partnership.

Choose a partnership you have coached before, one that you know will model the behaviors of providing the kind of feedback you want the rest of the class to learn and practice. Ideally, you'll set this up with the partnership beforehand, letting them know that they work so hard to support one another that you think the rest of the class could learn from them. This will provide confidence to the partnership while all eyes are on them, but also will help them focus on providing each other with feedback in a productive way.

ACTIVE ENGAGEMENT

Channel partners to give each other feedback.

"Writers, your partner is next to you. Do you think you could, right now, try some of that important partner work?" The class agreed.

"Great!" I said. "Get set up, decide who will give feedback and who will receive feedback, and then give it a try."

As partnerships started to work together, I walked around the outside of the circle and began coaching partnerships. I coached them to use the checklist to give feedback, reminding the partner providing feedback to give a compliment and something to practice. After one partner had gone through the cycle, I called the class back together.

LINK

Send writers off, reminding them that they can ask their partner for feedback or give themselves feedback if they need it.

"Writers, I know only one of you had time to receive feedback from your partner. As you set off to write today, know that you can ask your partner for feedback, especially if you haven't gotten any. But, remember, you can also give *yourself* feedback. You've done it before! Just use the checklist to find something that you can practice over and over."

When you coach partnerships, it is helpful to listen in from behind them and simply whisper coaching prompts into their ears. When you position your body behind a partnership, it prevents the kids from turning to talk to you instead of keeping their main focus on their partner, which is your goal. As you whisper prompts into a partnership, you are supplying them with language that they can use in your absence.

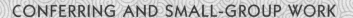

Utilizing Partners to Support Revision and Editing

TODAY'S MINILESSON encouraged partners to give each other precise feedback using the checklist. By now, most of your writers will be familiar with all of the tools and resources on offer—charts, mentor texts, the writing center, and the Information Writing Checklist. So perhaps during today's conferring and small-group work time, you'll focus your energy on helping students set up small groups in which they support each other. You could invite writers working on similar goals to gather together and make use of mentor texts as a resource. Partners could mine mentor texts for helpful strategies as they work to improve their own books. You might also invite writers working on the goal of improving their spelling to gather in a group and form partnerships to help with some of that editing work. Then again, you may have a handful of writers who need more one-on-one support prioritizing their goals and making a plan for their work.

If you notice several writers working toward a similar goal, you might pull them together and offer up mentor texts they can study to understand the ways mentors accomplish that same goal. Perhaps there are four or five writers working toward the goal of wrapping up their piece. They could study the ways authors of how-to books, question-and-answer books, and stories that teach wrap up *their* books. Writers working on the same kind of writing can partner up and share a mentor text. In this way, you will extend the use of partnerships and allow writers to rely on each other as resources instead of you. Partners may notice that how-tos wrap up with some tips or a little reminder of what the reader learned, while question-and-answer books tend to end with a bit of thinking or a big idea about the topic.

You might find that some writers are working toward making their writing more readable by improving their spelling. They will benefit not only from using the resources around the room and the spelling strategies from Session 12, but also from consulting with one another. You could gather a group of these writers together, inviting them to bring their white boards as well. Kids can use these as a work surface, writing and erasing their spelling tries before committing them into their books.

The small group may begin with you inviting writers to partner up with someone else in the group and then to read a page or part of one partner's book together, carefully circling any words that look like they could use more attention. You could offer up

---

MID-WORKSHOP TEACHING **Using the Information Checklist for Different Kinds of Nonfiction Books**

"Writers, can I call your attention to something for a moment? I saw many of you using the checklist to give feedback and practice goals. One thing I noticed is that even though you are writing new kinds of nonfiction books, you can *still* use the checklist to make your book the best that it can be. Can I give you a tip? As you're using the checklist, you can think, 'How does this goal look and sound in this *kind* of book?'

"Quickly, put your finger on the part of the checklist that says *Organization*. Let's read that part together." The class joined me in reading. "Think with the person next to you, if you were writing a how-to book, how would you organize your writing into different parts so that each part told different information about the topic? Turn and tell the person next to you."

After a moment I continued, "What if you were writing a story that teaches? Would you organize your book the same way?" The class agreed that you would not. "Hmm, . . . well, how *would* you organize a story that teaches so that there are different parts and each part tells different information about the topic? Turn and share." I gave another moment for the kids to talk.

"Writers, as you continue to use the Information Writing Checklist to set goals and practice them, remember to think, 'How does this goal look and sound in this *kind* of book?' Goals might look and sound a bit different in a how-to, a story that teaches, or a question-and-answer book."

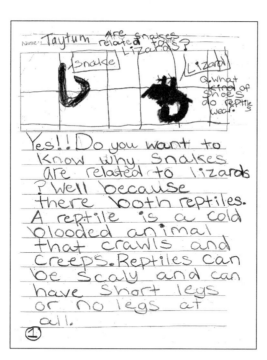

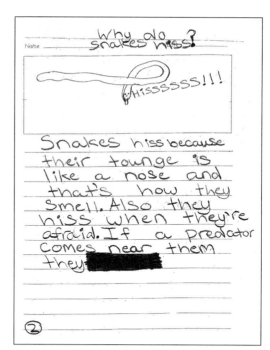

Why do
Snakes hiss?

By Taytum

Name: Taytum Are snakes related to lizards?

[Snake] [Lizard]
Q. What kind of shoes do reptiles wear?

Yes!! Do you want to know why snakes are related to lizards? Well because there both reptiles. A reptile is a cold blooded animal that crawls and creeps. Reptiles can be scaly and can have short legs or no legs at all.

①

Why do snakes hiss?

Name _____

Hisssssss!!!

Snakes hiss because their tounge is like a nose and that's how they smell. Also they hiss when they're afraid. If a predator comes near them they ▪▪▪▪▪▪

②

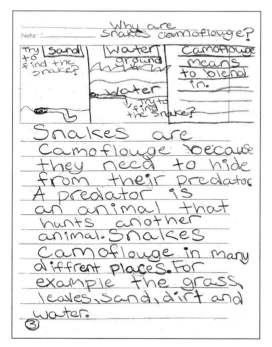

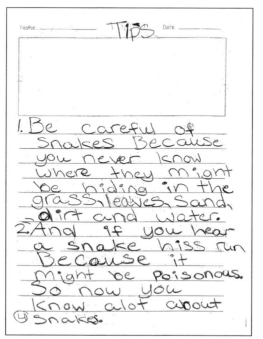

Name _____ Why are snakes camoflouge?

Try to find the snake? [Sand] [Water ground] [Camoflouge means to blend in.]
water
I try to find the snake?

Snakes are camoflouge because they need to hide from their predator. A predator is an animal that hunts another animal. Snakes camoflouge in many diffrent places. For example the grass, leaves, sand, dirt and water.

③

Name _____ Tips Date _____

1. Be careful of snakes Because you never know where they might be hiding in the grass, leaves, sand, dirt and water.
2. And if you hear a snake hiss run Because it might be poisonous. So now you know alot about snakes.

④

FIG. 17–1   Taytum chose the goal of elaboration so she revised to include different kinds of information across her question-and-answer book. She added an entire page of tips as well as a description at the end of page 1 and examples at the end of page 3.

reminders of the strategies they know, such as using parts of words they know to help them spell new words, clapping syllables, and trying a word three times before selecting the one that looks closest to the correct spelling. You might spend a bit of time coaching into these partnerships to ensure they make use of all of the tools available to them.

Other writers may need more one-on-one support, perhaps to prioritize goals from the checklist. You could remind them of the work they did in Session 11 around setting goals, and invite them to cut the checklist into goal flaps. You could then prompt them to pull off three or four goals and put them in order with the most-needed goal on top and the others to follow. Perhaps that means a writer will end up working first on "including words to show she is an expert on a topic," then moving to "organizing her book so each part teaches something different," and then end with checking her spelling. In that way, the writer can focus in on what specifically needs to be done to improve her books in an order of her choosing.

Making Choices and Preparing for the Final Celebration

Rally students for the upcoming celebration and channel them to choose the books they will publish. Emphasize that tomorrow will be their last workday.

"Writers, for today's share session you can stay at your writing spots because you will need some extra space to look through your folders. So pens down and eyes on me."

I waited for their attention. "Our celebration is only two days away! I am so excited and I bet you are, too. I was thinking that today you might want some time to make a plan for your last workday tomorrow. You have written several books across this unit, including some different kinds of books in the past week. So first you'll need to decide which books from this bend you want to celebrate. Go ahead and look across your books. You might move the ones you want to celebrate over toward the 'in progress' side of your folder."

I watched as students set books out on their tables and then made decisions. I made a mental note of a few students who seemed a bit unsure about their choices so I could work with them the next day.

"Now that you have a few books you plan on celebrating, take a closer look at each book and notice how much work each book will need tomorrow. You could study each book and ask, 'Does this book need a lot of work? Or does it just need a few finishing touches? If you're unsure, ask the person next to you to take a look and you can decide together." I moved from one table of writers to the next as kids reflected on the work each book might need.

"Tomorrow you can look back through the books you chose and make a plan for your work time. We're so close to our final celebration!"

This time for reflection and preparation is important. You will want to communicate to your students that the book they choose to share is truly up to them—they are in charge of their writing lives. Providing time for writers to plan for their work tomorrow will also allow you to gauge whether a day for preparation will be enough for most students or if they might need a bit more time finishing up their books before celebrating.

Planning for the Final Celebration

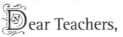ear Teachers,

During the share from the previous session, your students made plans for how they will get ready for tomorrow's celebration. Many writers may have decided to celebrate two or even three books, so today provides them with time to get those books in tip-top shape!

We imagine today will look like a busy workshop where kids get right to work so that they have time for final revisions, edits, and fancying up. You may decide to use the mini-lesson as a time to remind writers to make their own choices about their work time and to use the tools, charts, and partnerships that have supported them across this unit—now doing this with lots of independence. If you choose to support writers in this way, you could encourage them to make their own work plans, or to make little to-do lists, and then to meet with partners before heading off to work like the wind.

Your conferring and small-group work today will support writers in their plans. Perhaps you will make suggestions or offer tips, but you won't linger with any one writer for too long, since everyone will need to take advantage of their work time to accomplish their plans before tomorrow's celebration.

We suggest that by the end of today, you and your students will decide on a plan for the celebration. Of course, you can celebrate in any way you choose, but we suggest holding a learning expo. Your writers have worked hard to write books for others and in this last bend to write books in new ways. There will be so many different kinds of books for your class to share! It may be nice to set up a learning expo where guests can come and learn from the authors themselves. No matter how you choose to celebrate, don't forget to help writers plan for who will attend as well!

MINILESSON

In your connection, you may want to invite writers to gather all of the charts and tools they think will be helpful as they plan their last day of work on their books. You could invite them to scour the room and their folders for everything they think they will need to make the day a productive one. Kids will certainly lean on the anchor charts of the unit as well as their Information Writing Checklist. Some kids may grab mentor texts that they have apprenticed themselves to and will have those by their side as well.

With all of these resources front and center, you could then invite writers to make plans for their work today. Perhaps your teaching point sounds like this, "Writers, today I want to remind you that as writers get ready to publish, or celebrate their work, they lean on everything they know to ready their books. Writers sometimes find it helpful to make a little list of things they need to do to get their books ready for others. Then they work to make their books the best they can be!"

During the teaching, instead of demonstrating how you make your own plan, you could invite a student up to the front, and the class could work to help that student make a plan for his or her work time today. You may want to highlight how important it is for writers to look between their books and the resources at hand to make decisions about what will help them ready their books. Of course there are many things a writer does to ready his or her book for a celebration, but writers will only have this workshop to put on the final touches, so it will be important for them to determine what work is most important and to plan accordingly.

Then in the active engagement, writers could work to make their own plans. Maybe you remind them to look back at the books in their folders and then to look across the charts or at their checklist as a way to begin planning their work. Encourage your students to determine what is most important for their work today, and invite them to jot three or four big things they think they need to work on today on a Post-it.

In the link, writers might review their plans with their partners and decide on the tools they need before heading off to work on their to-do lists.

CONFERRING AND SMALL-GROUP WORK

We imagine your conferring and small-group work today will be led by the students. Allow them to lead your focus—after all, they have set forth a plan for their work today. You might want to begin your conferences and ask, "What are your plans? Can you show me what you've been doing? What are you planning to do next?" Then you can help them get started on something new from their to-do list or perhaps redirect their efforts if they seem off course. You may notice some writers rushing to check off each item on their plan instead of taking time to really work on making their books their best. These writers may benefit from a reminder of how they took care with one item from the checklist in Bend II and looked across their book to make sure they were working to make each chapter or part the best it could be. You could also suggest they partner up with another writer who is writing a similar kind of book, and work together to carefully check that each book is ready to go. The important thing is to have a workshop where all writers are engaged in readying their books for others and not sitting around waiting for tomorrow's celebration. On a day like today, it is unlikely you will find anyone not working away, but it's good to be ready and on the lookout for those kids just in case.

Mid-Workshop Teaching

You may have tucked the "Books Get Fancy! Preparing for Publication" chart from Session 13 away, after your celebration in Bend II, but now is a great time to get that out. You might say, "Writers, as you were looking around the room during the minilesson, and gathering resources to help you make your plans, I happened across this chart from our last bend. If you think your books are ready to get fancy, you might look back across this chart and add a few items to your to-do list!"

SHARE

You may decide to end your workshop today by thinking toward tomorrow's celebration. You could gather writers with their folders and share that tomorrow you will hold a learning expo. You could explain that an expo is a large exhibit where people often set up booths and present to guests of the expo.

You could then have students sort through all of their published books, deciding which book they will celebrate at the expo. It will be important for kids to think about who to invite and how they will let people know to come.

After a bit of discussion and decision making, kids may sign up to make signs to post in the hallway and around the school, alerting others of the learning expo. Other kids might take on the job of making invitations and sending them off. It will be a whole-class effort to prepare for tomorrow's celebration and it will be well worth it!

Best of luck,
Valerie and Jen

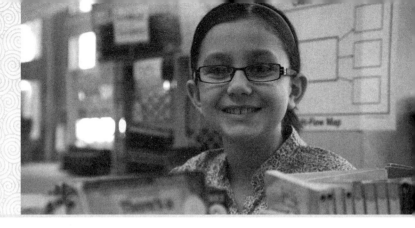

Session 19

Holding a Learning Expo

A Celebration of Nonfiction Authors and Their Work

THIS SESSION celebrates the work of your second-graders as this nonfiction unit comes to a close. They have taken quite a journey through this unit—first working to become like the nonfiction writers they have surely grown to admire, then working to write for an audience, and finally molding their expertise into new kinds of nonfiction books. At each step of the way, you encouraged your youngsters to write in ways that teach others and to share their expertise with the world.

Today's celebration—a learning expo—will showcase your second-graders' knowledge of expert topics and, most importantly, their ability to write different kinds of nonfiction books. We suggest that this final celebration involves a bit more fanfare than the others in this unit. We know you'll want to open up your classroom to audiences of all kinds— fellow second-grade classes, families, or schoolmates—to attend this learning expo, read the books your second-graders have worked so hard to create, and learn from the authors themselves.

Before the day begins, we recommend finding a space, a "booth," for each student. You might label these areas with each student's name ahead of time, making it easy for kids to prepare. To get ready for this celebration, you'll help youngsters think about how they can best celebrate the kind of writing they chose for the celebration. For example, children who are celebrating how-to books will likely want to teach each step, possibly by acting, while those who wrote question-and-answer books might set up an interview scenario. Children who are celebrating stories that teach may choose to act out their favorite parts or even perform a read-aloud, mimicking storytime. However children choose to celebrate their books, the goal is for their celebration to highlight all they've learned.

As students make plans, you'll want to be there to coach them to choose the best way to showcase the information in their book. You'll also want to make plenty of art materials available, so that kids will be able to make signs, props, costumes, and such to prepare for the expo.

When guests arrive at the learning expo, you'll guide them to walk from booth to booth, learning from students as they present their information in various ways and browsing

IN THIS SESSION, you'll teach children how to prepare for a celebration and hold a learning expo to celebrate.

GETTING READY

✔ Before this session, decide who you will invite as guests to the expo, and issue invitations.

✔ Find a space in the classroom for each child to use as a "booth" for the expo and label it with the child's name.

✔ Gather a variety of art materials so that students can make signs, props, or costumes to support their book presentations at the expo.

✔ Make space in the nonfiction section of your classroom library to receive your students' nonfiction books at the end of this session.

✔ Students should bring the books that they chose to celebrate in Session 18 with them to the meeting area (see Preparing to Celebrate)

✔ "How to Celebrate Different Kinds of Writing" one-day chart (see Preparing to Celebrate) ☚

through their books. Make sure you take time to visit the booths of your students, listening as they teach and watching with pride. To bring your celebration to a close, invite students to place their published books in the nonfiction section of your classroom library, bringing the unit full circle as you end with a full library.

PREPARING TO CELEBRATE

Recruit students to plan for a learning expo, deciding how to showcase the kind of writing they choose to celebrate.

"Writers, yesterday you picked a published book to celebrate. Will you bring it with you over to the rug?"

After a minute, the class was gathered. "In just a little bit, people will begin to come to our classroom to celebrate your efforts, so we'll need to take some time now to prepare for our learning expo. Each of you chose a book to celebrate— one of your how-to books, or question-and-answer books, or story-that-teaches books. As you've learned, each of these kinds of books is special, so I was thinking they would each need a special celebration."

I pointed toward the chart I had posted on the easel and invited the class to read it aloud with me.

"In just a moment, you'll gather with people who are celebrating the same kind of book as you. You can talk together and think about how you can celebrate that kind of book. You'll then have about fifteen minutes to organize your very own booth and to make anything you need to teach guests who come to our learning expo."

Coach groups of students who are celebrating the same kind of writing as they plan for their showcase. Channel students to set up their booth.

I directed students who were choosing each kind of book to a different area of the room to plan. As they planned I walked around to each group to lend support. I listened in to the how-to group as students decided to act out steps from each of their books as a way to celebrate. I leaned in to give a tip, "You might think about making props to help you teach each step so that the people who visit will be able to see clearly what you're teaching."

Students in the question-and-answer book group was busily writing their questions on index cards when I walked over. "We are going to have people interview us," Gayle explained. I nodded and added, "You'll probably need microphones then. Think about how you could make some."

Over in the stories-that-teach group, some kids were acting out parts of their story, while others were reading their books aloud, practicing to hold their own storytime. John ran over and asked, "Can we make costumes to act out our books? I need soccer gear!"

"Of course," I responded.

How to Celebrate Different Kinds of Writing

1. How does this kind of book teach?

2. How can I celebrate that kind of teaching?

3. What will the celebration look like?

After about five minutes, I called for the class's attention. "Writers, all of you are planning to celebrate your books in ways that truly showcase each kind of book. Our guests are going to learn so much! You have the next fifteen minutes to set up your book, make the signs, props, or costumes that you need, and rehearse how the celebration of your book will go. Find your name—that space will be your 'booth.' Back to work!"

THE CELEBRATION

Walk the room with guests, guiding them through the expo and listening in to students as they teach other.

As guests began to arrive, ready to learn from the experts in our classroom, they were greeted by students at their booths. I walked the room with our guests, relishing the expertise and confidence of each student. As I passed by Morgan, he was using his construction-paper baseball bat to teach people how to hit a baseball. "Then you wait for the baseball to be thrown by the pitcher. But, be careful! If it isn't a good throw, you can't swing," he explained.

Sasha, donning her construction-paper kitten ears and a long yarn-and-pipe-cleaner tail, was acting out the story of a cat growing up, while nearby, Andrew was being interviewed. "How do you pick a truck to buy?" his mom asked, reading from the stack of index cards set up at his booth. He steadied his microphone and began to teach.

Gather everyone back together. End the celebration by inviting students to place their published books in the nonfiction section of the library.

After guests had made their way from booth to booth, learning from our class of second-grade experts and browsing the published books that were on display near each writer, I gathered everyone for one last, yet momentous celebratory moment. "Writers, could you bring your published books over to the rug? Family and friends, feel free to join us."

When everyone was settled, I continued, "Writers, you need to do one last thing before our celebration comes to an end. To wrap up our celebration, you will each place your published book in the nonfiction section of our library. This is a big deal! Your books will now live alongside the nonfiction authors we know and love." I paused to highlight the importance of the moment.

"When I call your name, come up to the library with your book and place it in the bin of your choosing. Marilyn . . ."

With each name called, the room erupted in applause. After each book was placed in its new home, we all took one last moment to look over at our library, at shelves now filled with nonfiction books by class 203B authors, and brought our celebration, our unit, to a close.

The Dolphin Day

By Emilia

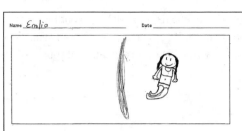

As Paige curled her toes in the sand and looked out into the ocean She saw it........ "Mommy, Mommy look, look" Paige exclaimed "What sweetie" Paiges mom laughed. Just then the intorcom said "Everyone get out of the water due to dolphin!" "Told you, Told you Mommy." Paige mocked "Woah. there is a dolphin, I think I know

①

Mom told paige
what Kind. "̂" How? there are over 350
Paige exclaimed
dolphins in this world!" "Well I think it's a Bottlenose because it's the most Common Dolphin in Rhode Island." Mom told Paige. "I want........" "Every-one get out of the water." The Intorcom rudley inturupting. "Well then
to do
what do you want" Mom questoined Paige. "I want"........ Paiges voice trailed off.

②

I want to go to the aquriam" Paige finished "Okay lets go" Mom anwserd. They quicley packed everyth-ing up and got into the car. In the middle of the car ride Paige asked "Mommy why do you think the dolphin came here? "Well mabey because the water is warm here in the summer and dolphins like warm water so it was able to swim up coast"

③

Mama anwserd. "Oh well that does mahe sense!" said paige. "Mommy when will we be there?" Paige Questoined "Right nnnowwww!" Mom anwserd as they aproched the parkinglot. "Yes!" Paige exclaimed. Paige ran out of the car and sprinted to the ticket booth. "Paige wait!" Mom shouted "Ok" Paige said breathlessly "But I want to see the dolphins".

④

As soon as mom got to the ticket booth mom pulled out her wallet and got out the money. She walked closer to the booth and talked into the speaker. It took ages for mom to get the wristb-ands. "Can we go to the dolphin exibit." Paige pleaded "Sure" mom anseu On the way there they

⑤

FIG. 19-1 Emilia's stories-that-teach book about dolphins. She wove facts about dolphins into a narrative to both entertain and teach.

saw two monkeys swinging together that made Paige laugh. After they saw the monkeys Paige saw a dolphin tank she rushed to it. She took a peek into the sighn in front of the tank and saw that she was looking at an atlantic spinner dolphin! "Mommy Mommy

⑥

look a spinner dolphin." Paige told her Mom "Wow, I havent seen one of these in a while, Do you know that they spin under water to get moumentou for when they breach?." Mom told Paige "What does breach mean mommy" Paige asked "Breach means like leap or shoot out of the water"

⑦

Mom anwserd. Paige turned around, and say "Woah look at that." Paige said a little too loudly. "Oh that is amazing" Mom exclaimed. Paige walked toared the tank "Brrr It's cold over here" Paige shiverd "It must be because the Orca lives in a colder habitat then the spinner" Mom told her.

⑧

"Oh thats seems right and this is also called a killer whale" Paige remarked "Woah look at the Emporor Penguin over there!" Mom exclaimed. "Umm can we keep looking at this first Because I want to figure out why they live in a colder habitat. Well actullay lets look at the

9

Emporor Penguin because I always love a good mystrey" Paige exclaimed!

10

FIG. 19–1 Emilia's stories-that-teach book about dolphins (Cont.)

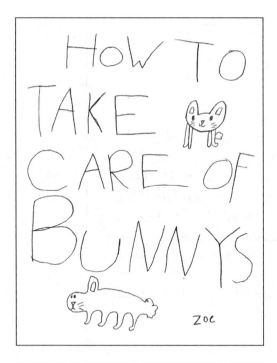

HOW TO TAKE CARE OF BUNNYS

Zoe

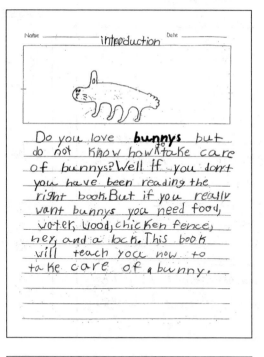

Introduction

Do you love **bunnys** but do not know how to take care of bunnys? Well if you don't you have been reading the right book. But if you really want bunnys you need food, water, wood, chicken fence, hey, and a lock. This book will teach you how to take care of a bunny.

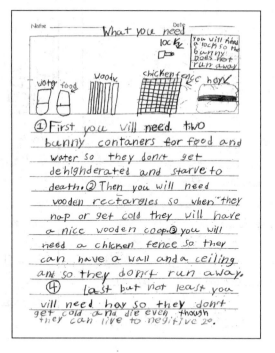

What you need

lock

You will need a lock so the bunny does not run away

water food woody chicken fence hay

① First you will need two bunny contaners for food and water so they don't get dehighderated and starve to death. ② Then you will need vooden rectangles so when they nap or get cold they will have a nice wooden coop. ③ you will need a chicken fence so they can have a wall and a ceiling and so they don't run away. ④ Last but not least you vill need hay so they don't get cold and die even though they can live to negitive 20.

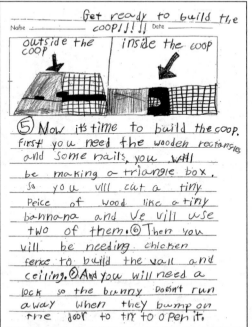

Get ready to build the coop!!!!

outside the coop | inside the coop

⑤ Now it's time to build the coop. First you need the wooden rectangles and some nails. you will be making a triangle box. So you vill cut a tiny peice of wood like a tiny bannana and Ve vill use two of them. ⑥ Then you vill be needing chicken fence to build the vall and ceiling. ⑦ And you will need a lock so the bunny Doesn't run away when they bump on the door to try to open it.

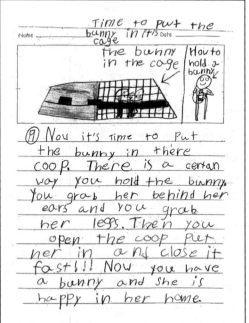

Time to put the bunny in it's cage

the bunny in the cage | How to hold a bunny

⑧ Now it's time to put the bunny in there coop. There is a certan way you hold the bunny. You grab her behind her ears and you grab her legs. Then you open the coop put her in and close it fast!!! Now you have a bunny and she is happy in her home.

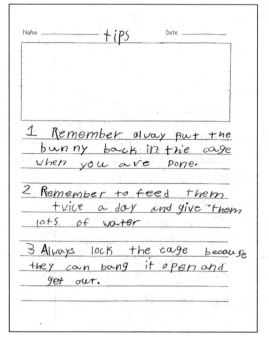

tips

1 Remember alway put the bunny back in the cage when you are done.

2 Remember to feed them tvice a day and give them lots of water

3 Always lock the cage because they can bang it open and get out.

FIG. 19–2 Zoe's how-to book teaches how take care of bunnies. She transfers elaboration strategies from Bend II to write for an audience.

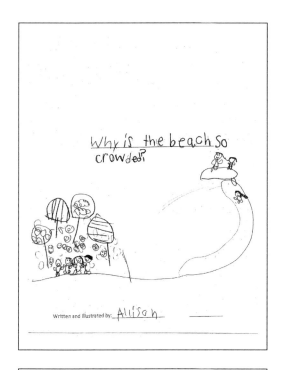

Why is the beach so crowded?

Written and illustrated by: Allison

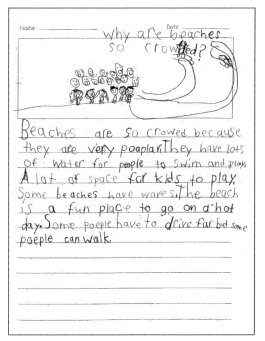

Why are beaches so crowded?

Beaches are so crowded because they are very poapular. They have lots of water for people to swim and play. A lot of space for kids to play. Some beaches have waves. The beach is a fun place to go on a hot day. Some poeple have to drive far but some poeple can walk.

What do you need for the beach?

You need an unbrela so you can sit in the shade. You need a bathing suit so you can go swiming. You need a beach chair so you can sit down. You can bring goggles to see hermit crabs and pretty shells. You need beach towels to dry your self off if you went swiming. You need a cooler full of food and drinks to last the hole day at the beach. Don't forget sun screen! If you don't put sun screen on you will get a sun burn. Now you are ready to spend the day at the beach!

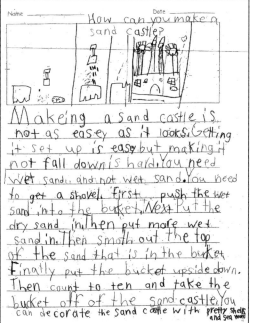

How can you make a sand castle?

Makeing a sand castle is not as easey as it looks. Getting it set up is easy but making it not fall down is hard. You need wet sand, and not wet sand. You need to get a shovel. First push the wet sand into the bucket. Next put the dry sand in. Then put more wet sand in. Then smoth out the top of the sand that is in the bucket. Finally put the bucket upside down. Then count to ten and take the bucket off of the sand castle. You can decorate the sand castle with pretty shells and sea weed.

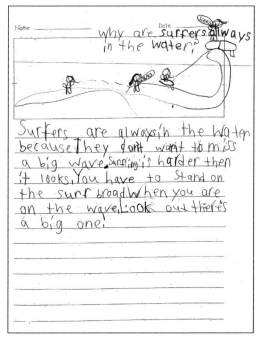

Why are surfers always in the water?

Surfers are always in the water because they don't want to miss a big wave. Surfing is harder then it looks. You have to stand on the surf broad when you are on the wave. Look out there's a big one.

FIG. 19–3 Allison's final piece reflects her ability to use questions-and-answer mentors to structure and develop her book.